Hebre

phrase book & diction

רְחוֹב הַיְּהוּדִים

حارة اليهود

JEWISH QUARTER St

Berlitz Publishing
New York   London   Singapore

...ted in any
...ithout prior

...but changes
...enience or
...outdated
...xpression not

Main

in our phrase book, please contact us at: comments@berlitzpublishing.com

Seventh Printing: January 2014
Printed in China

Head of Language: Kate Drynan
Design: Beverley Speight
Translation: Kwintessential
Contributors: Simon Griver
Production Manager: Vicky Glover
Picture Researcher: Beverley Speight
Cover Photos: © istockphoto

Interior Photos: APA Daniella Nowitz p.12,16, 21,33,36,39,73,102,108, 110,111,113,116, 128,137,142,149; istockphoto p.1,45,55,63,64,74,79,81,82,84,85,87,88,90,91,93,117,119 ,123,129,135,143,147,151,153,154,157,160,161,163,164,165,167; APA Robert Nowitz p.2 7,31,47,50,56,59,67,70,71,98,101,115,120,130,139,140,144; APA; APA Bev Speight p.49; APA Lynda Evans p.69; APA Britta Jaschinski p.77,86; APA Copenhagen p.89; APA Jerusalem p.112,118,121,131,132,133; APA Greg Gladman p.122,124; APA Abe Nowitz p.92,95;APA Corrie Wingate p.127.

Contents

Survival

Food & Drink

People

Leisure Time

Special Requirements

In an Emergency

Dictionary

Pronunciation

This section is designed to make you familiar with the sounds of Hebrew using our simplified phonetic transcription. You'll find the pronunciation of the Hebrew letters and sounds explained below, together with their 'imitated' equivalents. This system is based on sounds of familiar Hebrew words and is used throughout the phrase book. Simply read the transcription as if it were English, noting any special rules below.

Modern Hebrew has uniform rules of grammar (see p.170) and pronunciation, though its vocabulary is eclectic and draws on the Bible, medieval languages of the Mediterranean, and on modern scientific terminology. There is relatively little in the way of regional dialect, but Hebrew speakers or their ancestors may have brought with them from other countries special words for cultural specialties, such as food, dress, and social customs. It is worth nothing that speakers of Hebrew from a Middle Eastern background tend to stress the guttural sound of some letters more than those of European descent. The Middle Eastern pronunciation is considered to be the authentic ancient pronunciation.

Consonants

Letter	Approximate Pronunciation	Symbol	Example	Pronunciation
ב	**b** as in *bat*	**b**	בית	*bayit*
	or **v** as in *valley*	**v**	עבר	*avar*
ג	**g** as in *gate*	**g**	גן	*gan*
'ג	hard **j** as in *jeans*	**j***	ג'ינס	*jins*
ד	**d** as in *door*	**d**	דלת	*delet*
ה	**h** as in *have*	**h**	הר	*har*
ו	**v** as in *valley*	**v**	וריד	*vrid*
ז	**z** as in *zebra*	**z**	זית	*zayit*
'ז	soft **je** as in beige	**zh***	ז'קט	*zhaket*

ח	ch as in Scottish loch	kh	חמש	khamesh
ט	t as in tea	t	טלפון	telefon
י	y as in yet	y	יפה	yafe
כ	k as in king	k	כן	ken
	or ch as in Scottish loch	kh	יכול	yakhol
ל	l as in lip	l	לא	lo
מ	m as in mother	m	מלון	malon
נ	n as in never	n	נייר	niyar
ס	s as in sun	s	ספר	sefer
פ	p as in pot	p	פרח	perakh
	or f as in fan	f	ספל	sefel
צ	hard ts as in pots	tz	צמיג	tzamig
ק	k as in king	k	קפה	kafe
ר	r as in rain	r	ראש	rosh
ש	sh as in shine	sh	שמש	shemesh
	or s as in sun	s	שדה	sade
ת	t as in tea	t	תרמיל	tarmil

*The j and zh sounds have been introduced to cope with words of foreign origin.

Vowels

Strictly speaking, there are no vowels in unpointed Hebrew script (without the dots), and this is the script you'll see in this book. So you will find many words that appear to be made up of nothing but consonants. Even those letters that are technicaly semi-vowels – alef א, ayin ע, heh ה – are usually meant to be pronounced, effectively as guttural consonants.

Nevertheless, these letters are often silent and / or serve as vowels, mostly at the beginning or at the end of words. In addition, vav ו and yod י are proper consonants that are frequently used as vowels in order to aid pronunciation. Hebrew vowels tend to be short and flat, and rather more uniform than in English.

Letter	Approximate Pronunciation	Symbol	Example	Pronunciation
א	a as in *far*	a	ארון	*aron*
	or e as in *get*	e	ארץ	*eretz*
	or o as in *pot*	o	ראש	*rosh*
ה	a as in *far*	a	גבינה	*gvina*
	or e as in *get*	e	הרבה	*harbe*
ו	o as in *hot*	o	גדול	*gadol*
	or u as in *full*	u	זוג	*zug*
י	i as in *tin*	i	שמיכה	*smikha*
ע	a as in *far*	a	מרובע	*meruba*
	or e as in *get*	e	ערך	*erekh*

Stress

In Hebrew the stress tends to fall on syllables with long vowels, otherwise usually on the last syllable.

The Hebrew alphabet & script

The Hebrew alphabet is written from right to left, except numbers. For the alphabet, see the Dictionary chapter on p.181. The alphabet consists of letters, just like English, which are meant to remain separate, even in handwriting (though that is not always the case). Bear in mind that five letters take on a slightly different form at the end of a word, four of them by having a long downstroke. These are:

kaf (כ, ך)   mem (מ, ם)   nun (נ, ן)

pe (פ, ף)   tzadi (צ, ץ)

How to use this Book

> Sometimes you see two alternatives separated by a slash. Choose the one that's right for your situation.

ESSENTIAL

I'm here on vacation
[holiday]/business.

אני בחופשה/בנסיעה עסקית

ani bekhufsha/nesi-a iskit.

I'm going to...

... :אני הולך ל: ... / אני הולכת ל

ani holekh le:... m / ani holekhet le:... f

I'm staying at
the...Hotel.

... אני שוהֶה במלון... אני שוהָה במלון

ani shohe bemalon... m / ani shoha bemalon... f

> Words you may see are shown in YOU MAY SEE boxes.

YOU MAY SEE...

מכס	customs
מוצרים פטורים ממכס	duty-free goods
מוצרים להצהרה	goods to declare

> Any of the words or phrases listed can be plugged into the sentence below.

Tickets

A...ticket.	... כרטיס *kartis...*
one-way	הלוך *halokh*
round-trip [return]	הלוך חזור *halokh khazur*
first class	מחלקה ראשונה *makhlaka rishona*
business class	מחלקת עסקים *makhleket asakim*

Hebrew phrases appear in purple.

Read the simplified pronunciation as if it were English. For more on pronunciation, see page 7.

Bus

Do I have to change buses?	האם עלי להחליף אוטובוסים?
	ha-im alay lehakhlif otobusim?
Stop here, please!	תעצור כאן, בבקשה! / תעצרי כאן, בבקשה!
	ta-atzor kan, bevakasha! **m** / *ta-atzri kan, bevakasha!* **f**

For Tickets, see page 19.

Related phrases can be found by going to the page number indicated.

When different gender forms apply, the masculine form is followed by **m**; feminine by **f**.

Remember, Hebrew has a masculine and feminine form of "you" which means that the sentence changes slightly depending on whether you are talking to a man or a woman, irrespective of your own gender.

Information boxes contain relevant country, culture and language tips.

Expressions you may hear are shown in You May Hear boxes.

YOU MAY HEAR...

?לאן *le-an?*	Where to?
?מה הכתובת *ma haktovet?*	What's the address?

Color-coded side bars identify each section of the book.

Survival

Arrival & Departure

ESSENTIAL

I'm here on vacation [holiday]/business.	אני בחופשה/בנסיעה עסקית.
	ani bekhufsha/nesi-a iskit.
I'm going to...	אני הולך ל: ... / אני הולכת ל: ...
	*ani holekh le:... **m** / ani holekhet le:... **f***
I'm staying at the...Hotel.	אני שוהה במלון... אני שוהָה במלון ...
	*ani shohe bemalon... **m** / ani shoha bemalon... **f***

YOU MAY HEAR...

הדרכון שלך, בבקשה. הדרכון שלך, בבקשה. *hadarkon shelkha, bevakasha. **m** /* *hadarkon shelakh, bevakasha. **f***	Your passport, please.
מה מטרת הביקור שלך? מה מטרת הביקור שלך? *ma matrat habikur shelkha? **m** /* *ma matrat habikur shelakh? **f***	What's the purpose of your visit?
איפה תהיה? / איפה תהיי? *eyfo tihiye? **m** / eyfo tihiyi? **f***	Where are you staying?
כמה זמן תהיה? / כמה זמן תהיי? *kama zman tihiye **m** / kama zman tihiyi? **f***	How long are you staying?
עם מי תהיה כאן? / עם מי תהיי כאן? *im mi tihiye kan? **m** / im mi tihiyi kan? **f***	Who are you here with?

Border Control

I'm just passing through.	אני רק עובר כאן. / אני רק עוברת כאן. *ani rak over kan.* **m** / *ani rak overet kan.* **f**
I'd like to declare	אני רוצה להצהיר על ... / אני רוצה להצהיר על ... *ani rotze lehatzhir al...* **m** / *ani rotza lehatzhir al...* **f**
I have nothing to declare.	אין לי על מה להצהיר. *eyn li al ma lehatzhir.*

YOU MAY HEAR...

יש לך על מה להצהיר? יש לך על מה להצהיר? *yesh lekha al ma lehatzhir?* **m** / *yesh lakh al ma lehatzhir?* **f**	Anything to declare?
אתה צריך לשלם מכס את צריכה לשלם מכס. *ata tzarikh leshalem mekhes.* **m** / *at tzrikha leshalem mekhes.* **f**	You must pay duty.
פתח את התיק הזה / פתחי את התיק הזה. *ptakh et hatik haze.* **m** / *pitkhi et hatik haze.* **f**	Open this bag.

YOU MAY SEE...

מכס	customs
מוצרים פטורים ממכס	duty-free goods
מוצרים להצהרה	goods to declare
אין על מה להצהיר	nothing to declare
ביקורת דרכונים	passport control
משטרה	police

ESSENTIAL

Where's...?	**?איפה...** eyfo...?
the ATM	**הכספומט** hakaspomat
the bank	**הבנק** habank
the currency exchange office	**המשרד להמרת מט"ח** hamisrad lehamarat matakh
What time does the bank open/close?	**מתי הבנק נפתח/נסגר?** matay habank niftakh/nisgar?
I'd like to change dollars/pounds Sterling/Euro into shekels.	**אני רוצה להמיר דולרים/ לירות שטרלינג/ אירו לשקלים. / אני רוצה להמיר דולרים/ לירות שטרלינג/ אירו לשקלים.** ani rotze lehamir dolarim/lirot sterling/Ero lishkalim. **m/** ani rotza lehamir dolarim/lirot sterling/Ero lishkalim. **f**
I'd like to cash some traveler's cheques.	**אני רוצה לפדות המחאות נוסעים. אני רוצה לפדות המחאות נוסעים.** ani rotze lifdot hamkhaot nos'im. **m /** ani rotza lifdot hamkhaot nos'im. **f**

15

At the Bank

I'd like to change money/get a cash advance.	**אני רוצה להמיר כסף/לקבל מקדמת מזומן. אני רוצה להמיר כסף/לקבל מקדמת מזומן.** ani rotze lahamir kesef/lekabel mikdamat mezuman. **m /** ani rotza lahamir kesef/lekabel mikdamat mezuman. **f**

What's the exchange rate/fee?	?מה שער החליפין/שיעור העמלה
	ma sha'ar hakhalifin/she-ur ha'amla?
I think there's a mistake.	.אני חושב שיש טעות / אני חושבת שיש טעות
	*ani khoshev sheyesh ta-ut. **m** /*
	*ani khoshevet sheyesh ta-ut. **f***
I lost my traveler's cheques.	.איבדתי את המחאות הנוסעים שלי
	ibadeti et hamkha-ot hanos-im sheli.
My card...	...הכרטיס שלי *hakartis sheli...*
was lost	אבד *avad*
was stolen	נגנב *nignav*
doesn't work	לא פועל *lo poel*
The ATM ate my card.	הכספומט בלע את הכרטיס שלי
	hakaspomat bala et hakartis sheli

For Numbers, see page 174.

There are banks and bureaux de change everywhere and the exchange rates are the same in all of them. The New Israeli Shekel is stable and floats freely against the world's major currencies with a revised exchange rate each day.

YOU MAY SEE...

הכנס כרטיס כאן	insert card here
ביטול	cancel
נקה	clear
הכנס	enter
PIN	PIN
משיכה	withdraw
מחשבון עובר ושב	from checking [current] account
מחשבון חיסכון	from savings account
קבלה	receipt

YOU MAY SEE...

The official currency in Israel is the new sheqel ₪, divided into 100 agorot.
Coins: 10 agorot, ½ new shekel; 1 new shekel, 2, 5, 10 new shkalim
Notes: 20, 50, 100, 200 new shkalim

Getting Around

ESSENTIAL

How do I get to town?	?איך אוכל להגיע לעיר *eykh ukhal lehagi-a la'ir?*
Where's…?	?…איפה *eyfo…?*
the airport	שדה התעופה *sde hate-ufa*
the train station	תחנת הרכבת *takhanat harakevet*
the bus station/ stop	תחנת המרכזית\תחנת האוטובוס *takhanat ha-otobus/ takhanat hamerkazit*
the subway station [underground]	תחנת הרכבת התחתית *takhanat harakevet hatakhtit*
Is it far from here?	?זה רחוק מכאן *ze rakhok mikan?*
Where do I buy a ticket?	?איפה אפשר לקנות כרטיס *eyfo efshar liknot kartis?*
A one-way/ return-trip ticket to…	כרטיס הלוך\כרטיס הלוך חזור *kartis halokh/kartis halokh khazur…*
How much?	?כמה זה עולה *kama ze ole?*
Which gate/line?	?איזה שער/תור *eyze sha-ar/tor?*
Which platform?	?איזה רציף *eyze ratzif?*
Where can I get a taxi?	?איפה אפשר להשיג מונית *eyfo efshar lehasig monit?*
Take me to this address.	קח אותי לכתובת הזו. / קחי אותי לכתובת הזו. *kakh oti laktovet hazo.* **m** */ k'khi oti laktovet hazo.* **f**
Can I have a map?	?אפשר לקבל מפה *efshar lekabel mapa?*

Tickets

When's...to Tel Aviv?	מתי ... לתל אביב?	matay... Le-Tel Aviv?
the (first) bus	האוטובוס (הראשון)	ha-otobus (harishon)
the (next) flight	הטיסה (הבאה)	hatisa (haba-a)
the (last) train	הרכבת (האחרונה)	harakevet (ha-akhrona)
Where do I buy a ticket?	איפה אפשר לקנות כרטיס?	eyfo efshar liknot kartis?
One/Two ticket(s) please.	כרטיס אחד בבקשה. / שני כרטיסים בבקשה.	Kartis ekhad, bevakasha. / shney kartisim,
For today/tomorrow.	להיום/מחר בבקשה.	lehayom/makhar, bevakasha.
A...ticket.	כרטיס ...	kartis...
one-way	הלוך	halokh
round trip [return]	הלוך חזור	halokh khazur
first class	מחלקה ראשונה	makhlaka rishona
business class	מחלקת עסקים	makhleket asakim
economy class	מחלקת תיירים	makhleket tayarim
How much?	כמה זה עולה?	kama ze ole?
Is there a discount for...?	האם יש הנחה ל...?	ha-im yesh hanakha le...?
children	ילדים	yeladim
students	סטודנטים	studentim
senior citizens	גמלאים	gimla-im
tourists	תיירים	tayarim
The express bus/ express train, please.	אוטובוס אקספרס/ רכבת אקספרס, בבקשה.	otobus ekspres/rakevet exkspress, bevakasha.
The local bus/train, please.	אוטובוס מקומי/רכבת מקומית, בבקשה.	otobus mekomi/rakevet mekomit, bevakasha.
I have an e-ticket.	יש לי כרטיס אלקטרוני.	yesh li kartis elektroni.
Can I buy...	אפשר לקנות...	efshar liknot...
a ticket on the bus/train?	כרטיס לאוטובוס/רכבת?	kartis le-otobus/rakevet?

the ticket before boarding?	?...את הכרטיס לפני עליה על
	et hakartis lifney aliya la...?
How long is this ticket valid?	?לכמה זמן הכרטיס הזה תקף
	lekama zman hakartis haze takef?
Can I return on the same ticket?	?האם אפשר לחזור באמצעות אותו הכרטיס
	ha-im efshar lakhazor be-emtzaut oto hakartis?
I'd like to... my reservation.	.אני רוצה ... את ההזמנה שלי
	.אני רוצה ... את ההזמנה שלי
	ani rotze ... et ha-hazmana sheli. **m**
	ani rotza ... et ha'hazmana sheli. **f**
cancel	לבטל *levatel*
change	לשנות *leshanot*
confirm	לאשר *le-asher*

For Days, see page 176.

Plane

Airport Transfer

How much is a taxi to the airport?	?כמה עולה מונית לשדה התעופה
	kama ola monit lisde hate-ufa?
To...Airport, please.	.שדה התעופה ..., בבקשה
	lisde hate-ufa ... bevakasha.
My airline is...	....חברת התעופה שלי היא *khevrat hate-ufa sheli hi....*
My flight leaves at...	...הטיסה שלי עוזבת בשעה *hatisa sheli ozevet besha-a*
I'm in a rush.	אני ממהר / אני ממהרת. *ani memaher.* **m** /
	ani memaheret. **f**
Can you take an alternate route?	?אתה יכול לקחת נתיב חלופי
	?את יכולה לקחת נתיב חלופי
	ata yakhol lakakhat nativ khalufi? **m** / *at yekhola*
	lakakhat nativ khalufi? **f**

DEPARTURES

DESTINATION	הערות REMARKS	משוער ESTIM.	מתוכנן PLANNED	סוג TRAIN	רציף PLAT.
KEFAR-SAVA					
ASHQELON					
ḤAIFA		18:34	18:34	פרברית	
MODIIN		18:41	18:41	פרברית	5
NETANYA		18:42	18:42		
		18:	18:4		

YOU MAY HEAR...

עם איזו חברת תעופה אתה טס?
עם איזו חברת תעופה את טסה? /
im eyzo khevrat te-ufa ata tas? **m** /
im eyzo khevrat te-ufa at tasa? **f**

What airline are you flying?

פנימית או בינלאומית?
pnimit o beInle-umit?

Domestic or International?

איזה טרמינל? eyze terminal?

What terminal?

Can you drive faster/slower?	אתה יכול לנסוע יותר מהר/לאט? את יכולה לנסוע יותר מהר/לאט? ata yakhol linso'a yoter maher/le'at? **m** / at yekhola linso'a yoter maher/le'at? **f**

Checking In

Where's check-in?	איפה הצ'ק-אין? eyfo hachek in?
My name is...	השם שלי... ne-meh-ne on...
I'm going to...	אני טס ל... / אני טסה ל... ani tas le... **m** / ani tasa le... **f**

I have...	...יש לי	yesh li...
one suitcase	מזוודה אחת	mizvada akhat
two suitcases	שתי מזוודות	shtey mizvadot
one piece	חתיכה אחת	khatikha akhat
How much luggage is allowed?	?כמה מטען מותר	kama mit-an mutar?
Is that pounds or kilos?	?זה בפאונדים או קילוגרמים	ze bepa-undim o bekilogramim?
Which terminal?	?באיזה טרמינל	be-eyze terminal?
Which gate?	?באיזה שער	be-eyze sha-ar?
I'd like a window/ an aisle seat.	אני רוצֶה מושב ליד החלון/המעבר / אני רוצָה מושב ליד החלון/המעבר	ani rotze moshav leyad hakhalon/hama-avar. **m** / ani rotza moshav leyad hakhalon/hama-avar. **f**
When do we leave/arrive?	?מתי נעזוב/נגיע	matay na-azov/nagi-a?
Is the flight delayed?	?האם הטיסה מתעכבת	ha-im hatisa mitakevet?
How late?	?עד כמה האיחור	ad kama ha-ikhur

For Time, see page 176.

YOU MAY SEE...

נחיתות	arrivals
המראות	departures
קבלת מזוודות	baggage claim
ביטחון	security
טיסות פנימיות	domestic flights
טיסות בינלאומיות	international flights
צ'ק-אין	check-in desk
צ'ק-אין לכרטיסים אלקטרונים	e-ticket check-in
שערי יציאה	departure gates

YOU MAY HEAR...

הבא בתור! haba bator!	Next!
הדרכון/הכרטיס שלך, בבקשה. הדרכון/הכרטיס שלך, בבקשה. hadarkon/hakartis shelkha, bevakasha. **m** /hadarkon/hakartis shelakh, bevakasha. **f**	Your ticket/passport, please.
אתה מפקיד איזשהן מזוודות? את מפקידה איזשהן מזוודות? ata mafkid eyzeshehen mizvadot? **m** / at mafkida eyzeshehen mizvadot? **f**	Are you checking in any luggage?
זה גדול מדי למטען אישי. ze gadol miday lemit-an ishi	That's too large for a carry-on [piece of hand luggage].
האם ארזת את התיקים האלו לבד? האם ארזת את התיקים האלו לבד? ha-im arazta et hatikim ha-elu levad? **m** /Ha-im arazt et hatikim ha-elu levad? **f**	Did you pack these bags yourself?
האם מישהו נתן לך משהו לקחת? האם מישהו נתן לך משהו לקחת? ha-im mishehu natan lekha mashehu lakakhat? **m** / ha-im mishehu natan lakh mashehu lakakhat? **f**	Did anyone give you anything to carry?

Luggage

Where is/are...? ‏...?איפה eyfo...?

the luggage trolleys העגלות של המזוודות ha-agalot shel hamizvadot

the luggage lockers תאי אכסון מטען ta-ey ikhsun mitan

the baggage claim קבלת המזוודות kabalat hamizvadot

There are few left luggage facilities in Israel due to security issues but there are some at Ben Gurion International Airport.

My luggage has been lost/stolen.	המטען שלי אבד/נגנב.	
	hamitan sheli avad/nignnav.	
My suitcase is damaged.	המזוודה שלי ניזוקה.	
	hamizvada sheli nizoka.	

Finding your Way

Where is/are...?	?איפה...?	*eyfo...?*
the currency exchange	לחילופי מטבע	*lekhilufey matbe-a*
the car hire	שכירת רכב	*skhirat rekhev*
the exit	היציאה	*hayetzi-a*
the taxis	המוניות	*hamoniot*
Is there...	...האם יש	*ha-im yesh...*
into town?	?לעיר	*la-ir?*
a bus	אוטובוס	*otobus*
a train	רכבת	*rakevet*
a subway	רכבת תחתית	*rakevet takhtit*

For Tickets, see page 19.

Train

Where's the train station?	איפה תחנת הרכבת?	
	eyfo takhanat harakevet?	
How far is it?	מה המרחק?	*ma hemerkhak?*
Where is/are...?	?איפה...	*eyfo...?*
the ticket office	משרד הכרטיסים	*misrad hakartisim*
the information desk	דלפק המודיעין	*dalpak hamodi-in*

YOU MAY SEE...

רציפים	platforms
מודיעין	information
הזמנות	reservations
חדר המתנה	waiting room
הגעות	arrivals
יציאות	departures

the luggage lockers	תאי אכסון מטען	
	ta-ey ikhsun mitan	
the platforms	הרציפים	*haretzifim*
Can I have a schedule [timetable]?	אפשר לקבל לוח זמנים?	
	efshar lekabel lu-akh zmanim?	
How long is the trip?	מה האורך של הנסיעה?	
	ad kama aruka hanesi-a?	
Is it a direct train?	האם זו רכבת ישירה?	
	ha-im zo rakevet yeshira?	
Do I have to change trains?	האם עלי להחליף רכבות?	
	ha-im alay lehakhlif rakavot?	
Is the train on time?	האם הרכבת עומדת בזמנים?	
	ha-im harakevet omedet bazmanim?	

For Tickets, see page 19.

The rail service covers most major cities (except for Eilat and Tiberias) and connect with the airport and central bus station. For more information on routes and prices, visit **www.rail.co.il/en**. There is no train service on Sabbath or on Jewish holidays.

Departures

Which track [platform] to…?	איזה רציף הוא ל...? *eyze ratzif hu le…?*
Is this the track [platform]/ train to…?	האם זה הרציף/רכבת ל...? *haim ze haratzif le…?*
Where is track [platform]…?	איפה רציף...? *eyfo ratzif…?*
Where do I change for…?	איפה אוכל להחליף ל...? *eyfo ukhal lhakhlif le…?*

On Board

Can I sit here/ open the window?	אפשר לשבת כאן/לפתוח את החלון? *efshar lashevet kan/lifto-akh et hakhalon?*
That's my seat.	זה המושב שלי. *ze hamoshav sheli.*
Here's my reservation.	הנה ההזמנה שלי *hine hahazmana sheli*

YOU MAY HEAR…

כרטיסים, בבקשה. *kartisim, bevakasha.*	Tickets, please.
את צריכה להחליף ב... אתה צריך להחליף ב... *ata tzarikh lehakhlif be…? m / at tzrikha lehakhlif be…? f*	You have to change at…
התחנה הבאה... *hatakhana haba'a…*	Next stop…

YOU MAY SEE...

תחנת אוטובוס	bus stop
בקש לעצור	request stop
כניסה/יציאה	entrance/exit
החתם את הכרטיס שלך	stamp your ticket

Bus

Where's the bus station/ stop?	איפה תחנת האוטובוס? *eyfo takhanat ha-otobus / takhanat hamerkazit?*
How far is it?	מה המרחק? *ma hemerkhak?*
How do I get to...?	איך אפשר להגיע ל...? *eykh efshar lehagi-a le...?*
Is this the bus to...?	האם זה האוטובוס ל...? *ha-im ze haotobus le...?*
Can you tell me when to get off?	תוכל להגיד לי מתי לרדת? / תוכלי להגיד לי מתי לרדת? *tukhal lehagid li matay laredet?* **m** / *tukhli lehagid li matay laredet?* **f**
Do I have to change buses?	האם עלי להחליף אוטובוסים? *ha-im alay lehakhlif otobusim?*

Buses are the easiest way to get around — services are regular and fares are reasonable. Egged (**www.egged.co.il/eng/**) and Dan (**www.dan.co.il/english/**) are the main companies.

Stop here, please!	תעצור כאן, בבקשה! / תעצרי כאן, בבקשה!
	ta-atzor kan, bevakasha! **m** /
	ta-atzri kan, bevakasha! **f**

For Tickets, see page 19.

Subway

Where's the subway station?	איפה תחנת הרכבת התחתית?
	eyfo takhanat harakevet hatakhtit?
A map, please.	מפה, בבקשה. *mapa, bevakasha.*
Which line for...?	איזה תור הוא עבור...? *eyze tor hu avor...?*
Which direction?	לאיזה כיוון? *le-eyze kivun?*
Do I have to transfer [change]?	האם עלי להחליף?
	ha-im alay lehakhlif?
Is this the subway to...?	האם הרכבת התחתית הזו היא ל...?
	ha-im harakevet hatakhtit hazo hi le...?
How many stops to...?	כמה תחנות ל...?
	kama takhanot le...?
Where are we?	איפה אנחנו? *eyfo anakhnu?*

There is only a very small subway station and service operating in and around Haifa.

Taxi

Where can I get a taxi?	איפה אפשר להשיג מונית?
	eyfo efshar lehasig monit?
Can you send a taxi?	אתה יכול לשלוח מונית? / את יכולה לשלוח מונית?
	ata yachol lishlo-akh monit? **m** /
	at yekhola lishlo-akh monit? **f**
Do you have the number for a taxi?	יש לך מספר להזמנת מונית?
	yesh lekha mispar lehazmanat monit? **m** /
	yesh lakh mispar lehazmanat monit? **f**
I'd like a taxi now/ for tomorrow at...	אני רוצה מונית עכשיו/ למחר בשעה.../
	אני רוצֶה מונית עכשיו/ למחר בשעה...
	ani rotze monit akhshav/lemakhar besha-a... **m** /
	ani rotza monit akhshav/lemakhar besha-a... (f)
Pick me up at...	תאסוף אותי בשעה... / תאספי אותי בשעה...
	te-esof oti besha-a... **m** / *ta-assfi oti besha-a...* (f)
I'm going to...	אני נוסע ל... / אני נוסעת ל...
	ani nose-a le **m** / *ani nosa-at le...* **f**
this address	כתובת הזו
	ktovet hazo
the airport	שדה התעופה
	sde hate-ufa
the train station	לתחנת הרכבת
	letakhanat harakevet
I'm late.	אני מאחר / אני מאחרת
	ani me-akher. **m** / *ani me-akheret* (f)
Can you drive faster/slower?	אתה יכול לנסוע מהר/לאט יותר?
	את יכולה לנסוע מהר/לאט יותר?
	ata yakhol linso-a maher/le-at yoter? **m** /
	at yekhola linso-a maher/le-at yoter? **f**

YOU MAY HEAR...

לאן? *le-an?*

מה הכתובת? *ma haktovet?*

יש חיוב נוסף לנסיעה לילית/משדה התעופה.
yesh khiyuv nosaf lenesi-a leylit/misde hate-ufa.

Where to?

What's the address?

There's a nighttime/
airport surcharge.

The **sherut** is Israel's own indigenous mode of transport.
Individuals share a cab or minibus, which can take up to ten
people at a fixed price, usually equivalent to the bus fare for the same
route. In most cities, **sheruts** depart from near the central station.

Stop/Wait here.	עצור/חכה כאן. / עצרי/חכי כאן.
	atzor/khake kan. **m** / *itzri/khaki kan.* **f**
How much?	כמה? *kama?*
You said it	אתה אמרת שזה יעלה... / את אמרת שזה יעלה...
would cost...	*ata amarta sheze ya-ale...* **m** /
	at amart sheze ya-ale... **f**
Keep the change.	שמור את העודף. / שמרי את העודף.
	shmor et ha-odef. **m** / *shimri et ha-odef.* **f**

Bicycle & Motorbike

I'd like to hire...	אני רוצֶה לשכור... / אני רוצה לשכור...
	ani rotze liskor... **m** / *ani rotza liskor...* **f**
a bicycle	אופניים *ofanayim*
a moped	טוסטוס *tustus*
a motorcycle	אופנוע *ofano-a*

How much per day/week?	כמה זה עולה ליום/שבוע? *kama ze ole leyom / shavu-a?*
Can I have a helmet/lock?	אפשר לקבל קסדה/מנעול? *efshar lekabel kasda / manul?*
I have a puncture/flat tyre.	יש לי פנצ'ר/תקר בגלגל. *yesh li pancher/teker bagalgal.*

Car Hire

Where's the car hire?	איפה שוכרים מכונית? *eyfo sokhrim mekhonit?*
I'd like...	אני רוצֶה... / אני רוצָה... *ani rotze... **m** / ani rotza... **f***
a cheap/small car	מכונית זולה/קטנה *mekhonit zola / ktana*
an automatic/ a manual	עם הילוך אוטומטי/ידני *im hilukh otomati/yadani*
air conditioning	מיזוג אוויר *mizug avir*
a car seat	כיסא בטיחות *kise betikhut*
How much...?	כמה זה עולה...? *kama ze ole?*
per day/week	ליום/שבוע? *leyom/shavua?*
per kilometer	לקילומטר *lekilometer*
for unlimited mileage	לקילומטראז' לא מוגבל *lekilometrazh lo mugbal*

YOU MAY HEAR...

?יש לך רשיון נהיגה בינלאומי ?יש לך רישיון נהיגה בינלאומי *yesh lekha rishyon nehiga beynle-umi?* **m** / *yesh lakh rishyon nehiga beynle-umi?* **f**	Do you have an international driver's license?
.הדרכון שלך, בבקשה. / הדרכון שלך, בבקשה *hadarkon shelkha, bevakasha.* **m** / *hadarkon shelakh, bevakasha.* **f**	Your passport, please.
?אתה רוצֶה ביטוח? / את רוצה ביטוח *ata rotze bitu-akh?* **m** / *at rotza bitu-akh?* **f**	Do you want insurance?
.צריך הפקדה *tzarikh hafkada.*	I'll need a deposit. Initial/Sign here.
.תחתום/ראשי תיבות כאן .תחתמי/ראשי תיבות כאן / *takhatom/rashey tevot kan.* **m** / *takhtemi/rashey tevot kan.* **f**	

with insurance	עם ביטוח *im bitu-akh*
Are there any discounts?	?יש איזשהן הנחות *yesh eyzeshehen hanakhot?*

YOU MAY SEE...

דלק	gas [petrol]
נטול עופרת	unleaded
רגיל	regular
סופר	premium [super]
דיזל	diesel

Fuel Station

Where's the	איפה תחנת הדלק?
fuel station?	*eyfo takhanat hadelek?*
Fill it up.	למלא את המכל.
	lemale et hamekhal.
...shekel, please.	שקל, בבקשה. *shekel, bevakasha.* ......
I'll pay in cash/	אני אשלם במזומן/בכרטיס אשראי
by credit card.	*ani ashalem bemezuman/bekartis ashray.*

For Numbers, see page 174.

Asking Directions

Is this the way	האם זו הדרך ל...?
to...?	*ha-im zu haderekh le...?*
How far is it to...?	עד כמה רחוק זה ל...?
	ad kama rakhok ze le...?
Where's...?	איפה ze...? *eyfo*
...Street	רחוב... *rehov...*
this address	הכתובת הזו
	haktovet hazo
the highway	הכביש המהיר
[motorway]	*hakvish hama-ir*

There is no standardised spelling of Israeli place names. One might be **"Acre"** or **"Akko"** or even **"Acco"** or **"Elat, Elath** or **Eilat"** – so bear this in mind when you are looking at maps and road signs.

YOU MAY HEAR...

ישר *yashar*	straight ahead
שמאלה *smola*	left
ימינה *yamina*	right
מעבר לפינה *me-ever lapina*	around the corner
מול *mul*	opposite
מאחורי *me-akhorey*	behind
ליד *leyad*	next to
אחרי *akharey*	after
צפון/דרום *tzafon/darom*	north/south
מזרח/מערב *mizrakh/ma-arav*	east/west
ברמזור *baramzor*	at the traffic light
בצומת *batzomet*	at the intersection

Can you show me on the map?	אפשר להראות לי במפה? *efshar lehar-ot li bamapa?*
I'm lost.	הלכתי לאיבוד. *halakhti Le-ibud.*

Parking

Can I park here?	אפשר להחנות כאן? *efshar lehakhanot kan?*
Where's...?	איפה...? *eyfo...?*

the parking garage	חניון	*khenyon*
the parking lot [car park]	מגרש החניה	*migrash hakhanaya*
the parking meter	המדחן	*hamadkhan*
How much…?	?...כמה זה עולה	*kama ze ole…?*
per hour	לשעה	*lesha-a*
per day	ליום	*leyom*
for overnight	למשך הלילה	*lemeshekh halayla*

YOU MAY SEE...

STOP	stop	
תן זכות קדימה	yield	
אין חניה	no parking	
חד סטרי	one way	
אין כניסה	no entry	
הכניסה לרכבים אסורה	no vehicles allowed	
החצייה אסורה	no passing	
רמזור בהמשך	traffic signals ahead	
יציאה	exit	

Parking is difficult in the major city centres and it is best to look for a parking lot. If a curbside is marked in blue and white, you need a ticket, which you can purchase from stores or from streetside machines. Each ticket allows you to park for one hour. You must tear out the right time, month and day and display the ticket on the curbside window. This ticket system is in operation from 8:00 a.m. to 6:00 or 8:00 p.m. Outside of these hours, parking is usually free. Note that clamping and heavy fines are in operation along red and white marked curbsides and where there are No Parking signs.

Breakdown & Repair

My car broke down/ won't start.	**המכונית שלי התקלקלה/לא מניעה.** *hamekhonit sheli hitkalkela/lo matkhila.*
Can you fix it (today)?	**אפשר לתקן אותה (היום)?** *efshar letaken ota (hayom)?*
When will it be ready?	**מתי זה יהיה מוכן?** *matay ze ihiye mukhan?*
How much?	**כמה זה עולה?** *kama ze ole?*

Accidents

There was an accident.	קרתה תאונה. *karta te-una*
Call an ambulance/ the police.	צריך לקרוא לאמבולנס/למשטרה. *tzarikh likro le-ambulans/lamishtara.*

Places to Stay

ESSENTIAL

Can you recommend a hotel?	אתה יכול להמליץ על בית מלון? את יכולה להמליץ על בית מלון? *ata yakhol lehamlitz al beyt malon?* **m** / *at yekhola lehamlitz al beyt malon?* **f**
I made a reservation.	יש לי הזמנה. *yesh li hazmana.*
My name is...	השם שלי הוא... *hashem sheli hu...*
Do you have a room..?	יש לכם חדר? *yesh lakhem kheder?*
for one/two	לאחד/לזוג *le-ekhad/lezug*
with a bathroom	עם שירותים *im sherutim*
with air conditioning	עם מיזוג אוויר *im mizug avir*
For...	עבור... *avor...*
tonight	הלילה *halayla*
two nights	שני לילות *shney leylot*
one week	שבוע אחד *shavu-a ekhad*
How much?	כמה זה עולה? *kama ze ole?*
Is there anything cheaper?	יש משהו יותר זול? *yesh mashehu yoter zol?*
When's checkout?	מתי הצ'ק-אאוט? *matay ha "check out"?*
Can I leave this in the safe?	אפשר להשאיר את זה בכספת? *efshar lehash-ir et ze bakasefet?*

Can I leave my bags?	?אפשר להשאיר את התיקים שלי *efshar lehash-ir et hatikim sheli?*
Can I have my bill/ a receipt?	?אפשר לקבל את החשבון/הקבלה שלי *efshar lekabel et hakheshbon/hakabala sheli?*
I'll pay in cash/ by credit card.	אני אשלם במזומן/כרטיס אשראי. *ani ashalem bemezuman/bekartis ashray.*

Somewhere to Stay

Can you recommend…?	?...אתה יכול להמליץ על / ?...את יכולה להמליץ על *ata yakhol lehamlitz al…? m /* *at yekhola lehamlitz al…? f*
a hotel	מלון *malon*
a hostel	אכסניה *akhsaniya*
a campsite	אתר מחנאות *atar Makhana-ut*
a bed and breakfast (B&B)	לינה וארוחת בוקר *lina ve-arukhat boker*
What is it near?	?מה קרוב לזה *ma karov leze?*
How do I get there?	?איך אוכל להגיע לשם *eykh ukhal lehagi-a lesham?*

At the Hotel

I I have a reservation.	יש לי הזמנה *yesh li hazmana*
My name is…	...השם שלי הוא *hashem sheli hu…*
Do you have a room..?	?...יש לכם חדר *yesh lakhem kheder…?*
with a toilet/shower	עם שירותים/מקלחת *im sherutim/miklakhat*
with air conditioning	עם מיזוג אוויר *im mizug avir*
that's smoking/ non-smoking	שהוא למעשנים/לא מעשנים *shehu Leme-ashnim/lo me-ashnim*

For...	עבור... *avur...*
tonight	הלילה *halayla*
two nights	שני לילות *shney leylot*
a week	שבוע *shavu-a*
Do you have...?	?יש לכם... *yesh lakhem...?*
a computer	מחשב *makhshev*
an elevator [a lift]	מעלית *ma-alit*
(wireless) internet service	שירות אינטרנט אלחוטי *sherut internet alkhuti*

There is a wide choice of places to stay in Israel, but many of the modern, new establishments can lack charm. B&Bs are increasingly popular but for a more unusual taste of Israel, try **kibbutz** guesthouses or **kibbutzim**, which tend to be quite rural (**www.kibbutz.co.il**) or Christian hospices — more luxurious than they sound and usually with a 19th-century European ambiance. For a full list of hospices around the country, contact the Ministry of Tourism, **www.holyland-pilgrimage.org**.

YOU MAY HEAR...

הדרכון/כרטיס האשראי שלך, בבקשה. הדרכון/כרטיס האשראי שלך, בבקשה. *hadarkon/kartis ha-ashray shelkha, bevakasha.* **m** / *hadarkon/kartis ha-ashray shelakh, bevakasha.* **f**	Your passport/credit card, please.
מלא את הטופס הזה. / מלאי את הטופס הזה. *male et hatofes haze.* **m** / *mal-i et hatofes haze.* **f**	Fill out this form.
תחתום כאן. / תחתמי כאן. *takhatom kan.* **m** / *takhtemi kan.* **f**	Sign here.

room service	שירות חדרים *sherut khadarim*
a pool	בריכה *brekha*
a gym	חדר כושר *kheder kosher*
I need...	אני צריך... / אני צריכה... *ani tzarikh...* **m** / *ani tzrikha...* **f**
an extra bed	מיטה נוספת *mita nosefet*
a cot	מיטה מתקפלת *mita mitkapelet*
a crib	עריסה *arisa*

For Numbers, see page 174.

Tipping hotel staff such as porters a few shekels for each item of baggage is customary.

Price

How much per night/week?	?כמה זה עולה ללילה/לשבוע *kama ze ole lelayla/leshavu-a?*
Does that include breakfast/tax?	?האם זה כולל ארוחת בוקר/מס *ha-im ze kolel arukhat boker/mas?*
Are there any discounts?	?האם יש איזשהן הנחות *ha-im yesh eyzeshehen hanakhot?*

Preferences

Can I see the room?	?אפשר לראות את החדר *efshar lir-ot et hakheder?*
I'd like a...room.	...אני רוצה חדר *ani rotze kheder... m / ani rotza kheder... f*
better	יותר טוב *yoter tov*
bigger	יותר גדול *yoter gadol*
cheaper	יותר זול *yoter zol*
quieter	שקט יותר *shaket yoteer*
I'll take it.	אני אקח את זה *ani ekakh et ze.*
No, I won't take it.	לא, אני לא אקח את זה *lo, ani lo ekakh et ze.*

Questions

Where is/are...?	?...איפה *eyfo...?*
the bar	הבר *habar*
the bathrooms	השירותים *hasherutim*
the elevator [lift]	המעלית *hama-alit*
I'd like...	...אני רוצה / ...אני רוצֶה *ani rotze... m / ani rotza... f*
a blanket	שמיכה *smikha*
an iron	מגהץ *maghetz*
the room	את המפתח/כרטיס המפתח *et hamafte-akh/kartis hamafte-akh*
key/key card	של החדר *shel hakheder*
a pillow	כרית *karit*
soap	סבון *sabon*

toilet paper	נייר טואלט *Neyar toalet*
a towel	מגבת *megevet*
Do you have an adapter for this?	?האם יש לכם מתאם לזה *ha-im yesh lakhem mat-em leze?*
How do you turn on the lights?	?איך מדליקים את האורות *eykh madlikim et ha-orot?*
Can you wake me at…?	?...אפשר לקבל השכמה בשעה *efshar lekabel hashkama besha-a…?*
Can I leave this in the safe?	?אפשר להשאיר את זה בכספת *efshar lehash-ir et ze bakasefet?*
Can I have my things from the safe?	?אפשר לקבל בחזרה את הדברים שלי מהכספת *efshar lekabel bakhazara et hadvarim sheli mehakasefet?*
Is there mail /a message for me?	?האם קיבלתי דואר/הודעות *ha-im kibalti do-ar/hoda'ot?*
Do you have a laundry service?	?האם יש לכם שירות כביסה *ha-im yesh lakhem sherut kvisa?*

YOU MAY SEE…

לחץ/משוך	push/pull
שירותים	bathroom [toilet]
מקלחות	shower
מעלית	elevator [lift]
מדרגות	stairs
מכונות מכירה	vending machines
קרח	ice
כביסה	laundry
לא להפריע	do not disturb
דלת חסינת אש	fire door
יציאת חירום	emergency/fire exit
שיחת השכמה	wake-up call

Israel runs on 220-volt electricity, and most plugs are three-pronged, but you will come across two-pronged ones too. Converters and/or adapters can be purchased throughout the country.

Problems

There's a problem.	יש בעיה.	yesh be-aya.
I lost my key/key card.	איבדתי את המפתח/כרטיס המפתח שלי.	ibadeti et hamafte-akh/kartis hamafte-akh sheli.
I've locked my key/ key card in the room.	נעלתי את המפתח/כרטיס המפתח שלי בחדר.	na'alti et hamafte-akh/kartis hamafte-akh bakheder sheli.
There's no hot water/toilet paper.	אין מים חמים/נייר טואלט.	eyn ma-im khamim/neyar to-alet.
The room is dirty.	החדר מלוכלך.	hakheder melukhlakh.
There are bugs. in the room	יש חרקים בחדר. yesh kharakim bakheder.	
the air conditioning	המיזוג אוויר	hamizug avir
the fan	המאוורר	hame-avrer
the heat [heating]	החימום	hakhimum
the light	האור	ha-or
the TV	הטלוויזיה	hatelevizia
the toilet	בית השימוש	beyt hashimush
...doesn't work.	... לא פועל. / ... לא פועלת	lo po-el. *m* / lo po-elet. *f*
Can you fix...?	אתם יכולים לתקן...?	atem yekholim letaken...?
I'd like another room.	אני רוצה חדר אחר. / אני רוצה חדר אחר.	ani rotze kheder akher. *m* / ani rotza kheder akher. *f*

Checking Out

When's checkout?	?מתי הצ'ק-אאוט	matay hachek a-ut?
Can I leave my bags here until...?	?...אפשר להשאיר את התיקים כאן עד	efshar lehash-ir et hatikim kan ad...?
Can I have an itemized bill/ a receipt?	?אפשר לקבל חשבון מפורט/קבלה	efshar lekabel khesbon meforat/kabala?
I think there's a mistake.	.נראה לי שיש טעות	nir-a li sheyesh taut.
I'll pay in cash/by credit card.	.אני אשלם במזומן/בכרטיס אשראי	ani ashalem bemezuman/bekartis ashray.

Renting

I reserved an apartment/a room.	.הזמנתי דירה/חדר	hizmanti dira/kheder.
My name is...	...השם שלי הוא	hashem sheli hu...
Can I have the keys?	?אפשר לקבל את המפתחות	efshar lekabel et hamaftekhot?
Are there...?	?...יש	yesh...?
dishes	כלים	kelim
pillows	כריות	kariyot
sheets	סדינים	sdinim
towels	מגבות	magavot
kitchen utensils	כלי מטבח	kley mitbakh
When do I put out the bins /recycling?	?איפה בחוץ צריך לשים את פחי האשפה/המיחזור	eyfo bakhutz tzarikh lasim et pakhey ha-ashpa/hamikhzur?
...is broken.	מקולקל	mekulkal.
How does...	?...איך פועל ה	ekh po-el...?
work?		
the air conditioner	המזגן	hamazgan

the dishwasher	מדיח הכלים	*medi-akh hakelim*
the freezer	המקפיא	*hamakpi*
the heater	החימום	*hakhimum*
the microwave	המיקרוגל	*hamikrogal*
the refrigerator	המקרר	*hamekarer*
the stove	התנור	*hatanur*
the washing machine	מכונת הכביסה	*mekhonat hakvisa*

For In the Kitchen, see page 76.

Domestic Items

I need...	...אני צריך / אני צריכה...	
		ani tzarikh... **m** / *ani tzrikha...* **f**
an adapter	מתאם	*matem*
aluminum foil	נייר אלומיניום	*neyar aluminyum*
a bottle opener	פותחן בקבוקים	*potkhan bakbukim*
a broom	מטאטא	*matate*
a can opener	פותחן פחית שימורים	*potkhan pakhit shimurim*
cleaning supplies	חומרי ניקוי	*khomrey nikuy*
a corkscrew	חולץ פקקים	*kholetz pkakim*
detergent	חומרי ניקוי	*khomrey nikuy*

dishwashing liquid	סבון כלים	*sabon kelim*
bin bags	שקיות זבל	*sakiyot zevel*
a lightbulb	נורה	*nura*
matches	גפרורים	*gafrurim*
a mop	מגב	*magav*
napkins	מפיות	*mapiyot*
paper towels	מגבות נייר	*magavot niyar*
plastic wrap [cling film]	ניילון נצמד	*naylon nitzmad*
a plunger	פומפה	*pompa*
scissors	מספריים	*misparayim*
a vacuum cleaner	שואב אבק	*sho-ev avak*

For Oven Temperature, see page 180.

At the Hostel

Is there a bed available?	האם יש מיטה זמינה?	*ha-im yesh mita zmina?*
I'd like…	אני רוצֶה… / אני רוצָה…	*ani rotze… **m** / ani rotza… **f***
a single/double room	חדר ליחיד/זוג	*kheder leyakhid/zug*
a blanket	שמיכה	*smikha*
a pillow	כרית	*karit*
sheets	סדינים	*sdinim*
a towel	מגבת	*magevet*
Do you have lockers?	האם יש לכם תאי אחסון?	*ha-im yesh lakhem taey ikhsun?*
When do you lock up?	מתי אתם נועלים?	*matay atem sogrim?*

Do I need a membership card?	?האם צריך כרטיס חברות
	ha-im tzarikh kartis khaverut?
Here's my international student card.	.הנה כרטיס הסטודנט הבינלאומי שלי
	hine kartis hastudent habenle-umi sheli.

Going Camping

Can I camp here?	?אפשר לחנות כאן *efshar lakhanot kan?*
Where's the campsite?	?איפה אתר המחנאות
	eyfo atar hamakhana-ut?
What is the charge per day/week?	?מה החיוב ליום/לשבוע
	ma hakhiyuv leyom/leshavu-a?
Are there...?	?...האם יש
	ha-im yesh...?

YOU MAY SEE...

מי שתיה	drinking water
מחנאות אסורה	no camping
הצתת אש/ברביקיו אסורה	no fires/barbecues

cooking facilities	מתקני בישול *mitkaney bishul*
electric outlets	שקעים חשמליים
	shka-im khashmaliyim
laundry facilities	מתקני כביסה *mitkaney kvisa*
showers	מקלחות *miklakhot*
tents for hire	אוהלים להשכרה
	ohalim lehaskara
Where can I empty	איפה אפשר לרוקן את בית השימוש הכימי?
the chemical toilet?	*eyfo efshar leroken et beyt hashimush hakhimi?*

Communications

ESSENTIAL

Where's an internet cafe?	איפה יש אינטרנט קפה?
	eyfo yesh internet kafe?
Can I access the internet/check my email?	האם אוכל לקבל גישה לאינטרנט/לבדוק את הדוא"ל שלי? *ha-im ukhal lekabel gisha la-internet/livdok et hado-al sheli?*
How much per half hour/hour?	כמה זה עולה עבור חצי שעה/שעה? *kama ze ole avor khatzi sha-a/sha-a?*
How do I connect/log off?	כיצד אפשר להתחבר/להתנתק? *keytzad efshar lehitkhaber/lehitnatek?*
A phone card, please.	כרטיס חיוג, בבקשה. *kartis khiyug, bevakasha.*
Can I have your phone number?	אפשר לקבל את מספר הטלפון שלך? אפשר לקבל את מספר הטלפון שלך? *efshar lekabel et mispar hatelefon shelkha?* **m** / *efshar lekabel et mispar hatelefon shelakh?* **f**

Here's my number/email.	הנה המספר/האימייל שלי. *hine hamispar/ha email sheli.*
Call me.	תתקשר אלי. / תתקשרי אלי. *titkasher elay. **m** / titkashri elay. **f***
Email me.	שלח לי אימייל. / שלחי לי אימייל. *shlakh li Email. **m** / shilkhi li Email, **f***
Hello. This is…	שלום. מדבר… / שלום. מדברת… *Shalom. Medaber… **m** / Shalom. Medaberet… **f***
Can I speak to…?	אפשר לדבר עם…? *efshar ledaber im…?*
Can you repeat that?	אפשר לחזור על זה? *efshar lakhzor al ze?*
I'll call back later.	אני אתקשר בחזרה מאוחר יותר. *ani etkasher bakhazara me-ukhar yoter.*
Bye.	להתראות. *lehitra-ot*
Where's the post office?	איפה הדואר? *eyfo hado-ar?*
I'd like to send this to…	אני רוצה לשלוח את זה ל… / אני רוצה לשלוח את זה ל… *ani rotze lishlo-akh et ze le… **m** /* *ani rotza lishlo-akh et ze le… **f***

Telephone numbers made up of only a few digits preceded by
an asterix (e.g. Ben Gurion International Airport, tel. *6663) are
shortcuts that can be dialled on cellphones from within Israel.

Online

Where's an internet cafe?	?איפה יש אינטרנט קפה *eyfo yesh internet kafe?*
Does it have wireless internet?	?האם זה כולל אנטרנט אלחוטי *ha-im ze kolel internet alkhouti?*
What is the WiFi password?	?**Wifi** מה סיסמת ה- *ma sismat ha "Wi-Fi"?*
Is the WiFi free?	?בחינם **WiFi** האם ה- *ha-im ha "Wi-Fi" bekhinam?*
Do you have bluetooth?	?**Bluetooth** יש לכם *yesh lakhem "bluetooth"?*
Can you show me how to turn on/off the computer?	?אפשר להראות לי איך להדליק/לכבות את *efshar lehar-ot li eykh lehadlik/lekhabot et hamakhshev?*
Can I...?	?...האם אוכל *ha-im ukhal...?*
access the internet	להשתמש באינטרנט *lehishtamesh ba-internet*

check my email	לבדוק את האימייל שלי	*livdok at haemail sheli*
print	להדפיס	*lehadpis*
plug in/charge my laptop/iPhone/iPad/ BlackBerry?	לחבר/להטעין את המחשב הניש א /.../ שלי?	*lekhaber/lehat-in et hamakhshev hanisa /"iPhone/ iPad/BlackBerry" sheli?*
access Skype?	לקבל גישה ל-**Skype**?	*lekabel gisha le "Skype"?*
How much per half hour/hour?	כמה זה עולה לכל חצי שעה/שעה?	*kama ze ole lekol khatzi sha-a/sha-a?*
How do I...?	כיצד אוכל...?	*keytzad ukhal...?*
connect/disconnect	להתחבר/להתנתק	*lehitchaber/lehitnatek*
log on/off	להתחבר/להתנתק	*lehitkhaber/lehitnatek*
type this symbol	להקליד סמל זה	*lehaklid semel ze*

YOU MAY SEE...

סגור	close
מחק	delete
דוא"ל	email
יציאה	exit
עזרה	help
מסנגר	instant messenger
אינטרנט	internet
התחבר	log in
חדש (הודעה)	new (message)
דלוק/כבוי	on/off
פתח	open
הדפס	print
שמור	save
שלח	send
שם משתמש/סיסמה	username/password
אינטרנט אלחוטי	wireless internet

What's your email?	?מה האימייל שלך
	Ma haemail shelkha m shelakh f?
My email is...	...כתובת הדוא"ל שלי היא
	ktovet hado-al sheli hi...
Do you have a scanner?	?האם יש לכם סורק
	ha-im yesh lakhem sorek?

Social Media

Are you on Facebook/Twitter?	?**Facebook/Twitter** יש לך חשבון ב-
	?**Facebook/Twitter** יש לך חשבון ב-
	yesh lekha kheshbon befeysbuk/"Twitter"? m /
	yesh lakh kheshbon befeysbuk/"Twitter"? f
What's your username?	?מה שם המשתמש שלך / מה שם המשתמש שלך
	ma shem hamishtamesh shelkha? m /
	ma shem hamishtamesh shelakh? f
I'll add you as a friend.	.אני אוסיף אותך כחבר / אני אוסיף אותך כחברה
	ani osif otkha kekhaver. m / ani osif otakh kekhavera. f
I'll follow you	.**Twitter**-אני אעקוב אחריך ב/
	.**Twitter**-אני אעקוב אחריך ב
	ani e-ekov akhareykha be "Twitter". m /
	ani e-ekov akhara-ikh be "Twitter" f
Are you following...?	?...האם אתה עוקב / ?...האם את עוקבת
	ha-im ata okev...? m / ha-im at okevet...? f
I'll put the pictures on Facebook/Twitter.	.**Facebook/Twitter**-אני אעלה את התמונות ל
	ani a-ale et hatmunut lefeysbuk/"Twitter".
I'll tag you in the pictures.	.אני אתייג אותך בתמונות / אני אתייג אותך בתמונות
	ani atayeg otkha batmunut. m /
	ani atayeg otakh batmunut. f

Phone

A phone card/ prepaid phone, please.	כרטיס חיוג/כרטיס חיוג נטען, בבקשה. *kartis khiyug/kartis khiyug nitan, bevakasha.*
How much?	כמה זה עולה? *kama ze ole?*
Where's the pay phone?	איפה יש טלפון ציבורי? *eyfo yesh telefon tziburi?*
What's the area country code for…?	מהי הקידומת של המדינה/העיר עבור…? *mahi hakidomet shel hamedina/ha-ir avur…?*
What's the number for Information?	מה המספר למודיעין? *ma hamispar lamodi-in?*
I'd like the number for…	אפשר לקבל את את המספר של… *efshar lekabel et hamispar shel…*
I'd like to call collect [reverse the charges].	אני רוצֶה להתקשר/ אני רוצָה להתקשר גובינא *ani rotze lehitkasher govayna.* **m** *ani rotza lehitkasher govayna.* **f**
My phone doesn't work here.	הטלפון שלי לא פועל כאן. *hatelefon sheli lo po-el kan.*
What network are you on?	באיזו רשת אתה משתמש? באיזו רשת את משתמשת? *be-eyzo reshet ata mishtamesh?* **m** *be-eyzo reshet at mishtameshet?* **f**
Is it 3G?	האם זה 3G? *ha-im ze shalosh "G"?*
I've run out of credit.	נגמר לי האשראי/הדקות. *nigmar li ha-ashray/dakot.*
Can I buy some credit?	אפשר לקנות אשראי? *efshar liknot ashray?*
Do you have a phone charger?	יש לךָ מטען לטלפון? / יש לךְ מטען לטלפון? *yesh lekha maten latelefon?* **m** *yesh lakh maten latelefon?* **f**
Can I have your number?	אפשר לקבל את מספר הטלפון שלךָ? אפשר לקבל את מספר הטלפון שלךְ? *efshar lekabel et mispar hatelefon shelkha?* **m** *efshar lekabel et mispar hatelefon shelakh?* **f**
Here's my number.	הנה המספר שלי. *hine hamispar sheli.*

YOU MAY HEAR...

מי מבקש? / מי מבקשת?
mi mevakesh? **m** / *mi mevakeshet?* **f**

Who's calling?

רגע. *rega.*

Hold on.

אני אעביר אותך/אותך אליו/אליה.
ani a-avir otkha **m** *elav.* **m** /
ani a-avir otakh **f** *ele-a.* **f**

I'll put you through.

הוא/היא לא כאן/מדבר/מדברת בקו השני.
hu lo kan/medaber bakav hasheni **m** /
hi lo kan/medaberet bakav hasheni. **f**

He/She is not here/on another line.

את/ה רוצה להשאיר הודעה? *ata rotze lehashir hoda-a?* **m** / *at rotza lehashir hoda-a?* **f**

Would you like to leave a message?

תתקשר/י בחזרה יותר מאוחר/עוד עשר דקות.
titkasher bakhazara yoter meukhar/ od eser dakot. **m**
titkashri bakhazara yoter meukhar/ od eser dakot. **f**

Call back later/in ten mins

האם הוא/היא יכול/ה להתקשר אליך/אליך בחזרה?
ha-im hu **m** *yakhol* **m** *lehitkasher elekha* **m** *bakhazara?*/
ha-im hi **f** *yekhola* **f** *lehitkasher ela-ikh* **f** *bakhazara?*

Can he/she call you back?

מה המספר שלך/שלך?
ma hamispar shelkha? **m** /
ma hamispar shelakh? **f**

What's your number?

Please call/text me.	.תתקשר/שלח לי מסרון, בבקשה
	.תתקשרי/שלחי לי מסרון, בבקשה
	titkasher/shlakh li misron, bevakasha. **m**
	titkashri/shilkhi li misron, bevakasha. **f**
I'll call/text you.	.אני אתקשר/אשלח לך מסרון
	.אני אתקשר/אשלח לך מסרון
	ani etkasher/eshlakh lekha misron. **m**
	ani etshasher/eshlakh lakh misron. **f**

For Numbers, see page 174.

Remember, Hebrew has a masculine and feminine form of "you" which means that the sentence changes depending on whether you are talking to a man or a woman. So if you are talking to a man, follow the text marked with **m**, and if you are talking to a woman, follow the text marked with **f**.

Telephone Etiquette

Hello. This is…	שלום. מדבר… / שלום. מדברת… *shalom, medaber… m / shalom, medaberet… f*
Can I speak to…?	?…אפשר לדבר עם *efshar ledaber im…?*
Extension…	…שלוחה *shlukha…*
Speak louder/more slowly, please.	תדבר / תדברי בקול רם יותר/לאט יותר, בבקשה. *bekol ram yoter/le-at yoter, bevakasha.*
Can you repeat that?	?אפשר לחזור על זה *efshar lakhazor al ze?*
I'll call back later.	אני אתקשר בחזרה מאוחר יותר. *ani etkasher bakhazara me-ukhar yoter.*
Bye.	*lehitra-ot* להתראות.

Fax

Can I send/receive a fax here?	?אפשר לשלוח/לקבל פקס כאן *efshar lishlo-akh/lekabel faks kan?*
What's the fax number?	?מה מספר הפקס *ma mispar hafaks?*
Please fax this to…	…בבקשה לשלוח את זה בפקס אל *bevakasha lishlo-akh et ze befaks le…*

YOU MAY HEAR...

תמלא את טופס הצהרה למכס.
תמלאי את טופס ההצהרה למכס.
temale et tofes hahatzhara lamekhes. **m** /
temal'i et tofes hahatzhara lamekhes. **f**

מה הערך? *ma ha-erekh?*

מה נמצא בפנים? *ma nimtza bifnim?*

Fill out the customs
declaration form.

What's the value?

What's inside?

Post

Where's the post office/mailbox?	איפה הדואר/תיבת הדואר? *eyfo hado-ar/tevat hado-ar?*
A stamp for this postcard/letter to...	בול עבור הגלויה/המכתב הזה אל... *bul avor hagluya/hamikhtav haze el...*
How much?	כמה זה עולה? *kama ze ole?*
Send this package by airmail/express.	תשלחו את החבילה הזו בדואר אוויר/אקספרס. *tishlekhu et hakhavila hazo bedo-ar avir/ekspres.*
A receipt, please.	קבלה, בבקשה. *kabala, bevakasha.*

Post offices can be identified by a logo of a white stag leaping across a red background. Postboxes are red. As with most other places, post offices are closed Friday afternoon and on Saturday.

Food & Drink

Eating Out

ESSENTIAL

Can you recommend a good restaurant/bar?	אתה יכול להמליץ/ את יכולה להמליץ על מסעדה טובה / בר טוב?	*ata yakhol lehamlitz **m**/ at yekhola lehamlitz al misada tova/bar tov?* **f**
Is there a traditional /an inexpensive restaurant nearby?	האם יש מסעדה מסורתית/לא יקרה קרובה?	*ha-im yesh misada masortit/lo yekara krova?*
A table for..., please.	שולחן ל...., בבקשה.	*shulkhan le..., bevakasha.*
Can we sit...?	אפשר לשבת...?	*kan/sham*
here/there	כאן/שם	*bakhutz*
outside	בחוץ	*be-ezor shel lo me'ashnim*
in a non-smoking area.	באזור של לא-מעשנים	*minhsa'em ol lehs roze-eb*
I'm waiting for someone.	אני מחכה\מחכה למישהו	*ani mekhake **m** / ani mekhaka **f** le mishahu*
Where are the toilets?	איפה השירותים?	*eyfo hasherutim?*
The menu, please.	התפריט, בבקשה.	*hatafrit, bevakasha.*
What do you recommend?	על מה אתה ממליץ? / על מה את ממליצה?	*al ma ata mamlitz?* **m** / al ma at mamlitza* **f**
I'd like...	אני רוצֶה... / אני רוצָה...	*ani rotze... **m**/ ani rotza ...* **f**
Some more..., please.	עוד...., בבקשה.	*od..., bevakasha.*
Enjoy your meal!	בתיאבון!	*bete-avon!*
The check [bill], please.	חשבון, בבקשה.	*kheshbon, bevakasha.*

| Is service included? | זה כולל שירות? *ze kolel sherut?* |
| Can I pay by credit card/have a receipt? | אפשר לשלם בכרטיס אשראי/לקבל קבלה? *efshar leshalem bekartis ashray/lekabel kabala?* |

Where to Eat

Can you recommend...?	אתה יכול להמליץ / את יכולה להמליץ *ata yakhol lehamlitz* **m** / *at yelhola lehamlitz* **f**
a restaurant	על מסעדה *al misada*
a bar	על בר *al bar*
a café	על בית קפה *al beyt kafe*
a fast food place	מסעדת מזון מהיר *misedet mazon mahir*
a cheap restaurant	מסעדה זולה *misada zola*
an expensive restaurant	מסעדה יקרה *misada yekara*
a restaurant with a good view	מסעדה עם נוף טוב *misada im nof tov*
an authentic/ a non-touristy restaurant	מסעדה אותנטית/לא מכוונת לתיירים *misada otentit/lo mekhuvenet letayarim*

Reservations & Preferences

I'd like to reserve a table...	אני רוצה לשמור שולחן... / אני רוצה לשמור שולחן... *ani rotze lishmor shulkhan...* **m** / *ani rotza lishmor shulkhan...* **f**
for two	לשניים *leshnayim*
for this evening	לערב *lehaerev*
for tomorrow at...	למחר בשעה... *lemakhar besha-a...*
A table for two, please.	שולחן לשניים, בבקשה. *shulkhan leshnayim, bevakasha.*

I have a reservation.	יש לי הזמנה. *yesh li hazmana.*
My name is...	השם שלי הוא... *hashem sheli hu...*
Can we sit...?	אפשר לשבת...?. *efshar lashevet...?.*
here/there	כאן/שם *kan/sham*
outside	בחוץ *bakhutz*
in a non-smoking area	באזור של לא מעשנים *be-ezor shel lo meashnim*
by the window	ליד החלון *leyad hakhalon*
in the shade	בצל *batzel*
in the sun	בשמש *bashemesh*
Where are the toilets?	איפה השירותים? *eyfo hasherutim?*

How to Order

Excuse me, sir/ma'am?	סליחה, אדוני/גברתי? *slikha, adoni/gvirti?*
We're ready (to order).	סינכומ ונחנא .(להזמין) *Anakhnu mukhanim (lehazmin).*
The wine list, please.	רשימת יינות, בבקשה. *reshimat yeynot, bevakasha.*
I'd like...	אני רוצֶה... / אני רוצָה... *ani rotze...* **m** / *ani rotza...* **f**
a bottle of...	בקבוק... *bakbuk...*

YOU MAY HEAR...

יש לכם הזמנה?
yesh lakhem hazmana?

Do you have a reservation?

לכמה אנשים? *lekama anashim?*

How many?

מעשנים או לא-מעשנים?
me-ashnim o lo me-ashnim?

Smoking or non-smoking?

מוכן (להזמין)?/ מוכנה? / מוכנים? (רבים)
mukhan (lehazmin)? **m** / *mukhana (lehazmin)?* **f** / *mukhanim (lehazmin)? (plural)*

Are you ready (to order)?

מה תרצה? / מה תרצי?
ma tirtze? **m** / *ma tirtzi?* **f**

What would you like?

אני ממליץ... / אני ממליצה...
ani mamlitz... **m** / *ani mamlitza...* **f**

I recommend...

בתיאבון. *bete-avon.*

Enjoy your meal.

a carafe of...	קנקן... *kankan...*	
a glass of...	כוס... *kos...*	
The menu, please.	התפריט, בבקשה. *hatafrit, bevakasha.*	
Do you have...?	האם יש לכם...? *ha-im yesh lakhem...?*	
a menu in English	תפריט באנגלית *tafrit be-anglit*	
a fixed price menu	תפריט במחיר קבוע *tafrit bemekhir kavu-a*	
a children's menu	תפריט לילדים *tafrit liyladim*	
What do you recommend?	על מה אתה ממליץ? / על מה את ממליצה? *al ma ata mamlitz?* **m** / *Al ma at mamlitza?* **f**	
What's this?	מה זה? *ma ze?*	
What's in it?	מה יש בזה? *ma yesh beze?*	
Is it spicy?	זה חריף? *ze kharif?*	
Without..., please.	בלי..., בבקשה. *bli..., bevakasha.*	
It's to go [take away].	זה לקחת. *ze lakakhat.*	

For Drinks, see page 78.

YOU MAY SEE...

דמי כניסה	cover charge
מחיר קבוע	fixed price
תפריט (היום)	menu (of the day)
(לא) כולל שירות	service (not) included
מיוחדים	specials

Cooking Methods

baked	אפוי	*afuy*
boiled	מורתח	*murtakh*
braised	טיגון קל ולאחריו צליה	*tigun kal vle-akharav tzliya*
breaded	מצופה בפירורי לחם	*metzupe beperurey lekhem*
creamed	מוקצף	*muktzaf*
diced	קצוץ לקוביות	*katzutz lekubiyot*
filleted	מסונן	*mesunan*
fried	צלוי	*metuqan*
grilled	שלוק	*tzaluy*
poached	שלוק	*shaluk*
roasted	קלוי	*kaluy*
sautéed	טיגון קל	*tigun kal*
smoked	מעושן	*meushan*
steamed	מאודה	*meude*
stewed	מבושל	*mevushal*
stuffed	ממולא	*memule*

Dietary Requirements

I'm...	אני...	*ani...*
diabetic	סוכרתי / סוכרתית	*de-uh-beh-tick-oh*
lactose intolerant	רגיש למוצרי חלב / רגישה למוצרי חלב	
	ragish lemutzrey khalav **m** / *regisha lemutzrey khalav* **f**	

vegetarian	צמחוני / צמחונית	*tzimkhoni* **m** / *tzimkhonit* **f**
vegan	טבעוני / טבעונית	*tivoni* **m** / *tivonit* **f**
I'm allergic to…	...אני אלרגי ל... / אני אלרגית ל	
	ani alergi le… **m** / *ani alergit le…* **f**	
I can't eat…	...אני לא יכול לאכול... / אני לא יכולה לאכול	
	ani lo yakhol le-ekhol… **m** / *ani lo yekhola le-ekhol…* **f**	
dairy products	מוצרי חלב	*mutzrey khalav*
gluten	גלוטן	*gluten*
nuts	אגוזים	*egozim*
pork	חזיר	*khazir*
shellfish	רכיכות	*rekikhot*
spicy foods	אוכל חריף	*okhel kharif*
wheat	מוצרי חיטה	*mutzrey khita*
Is it kosher?	?האם זה כשר	
	ha-im ze kasher?	
Do you have…?	?...יש לכם	*yesh lakhem…?*
skimmed milk	חלב רזה	*khalav raze*
whole milk	חלב מלא	*khalav male*
soya milk	חלב סויה	*khalav soya*

---

i

Eating kosher is not always evident as many restaurants outside Jerusalem are not kosher. Outside of hotels, all kosher restaurants are closed on the Sabbath from sunset on the Friday, and during Jewish festivals.

Dining with Children

Do you have children's portions?	?יש לכם מנות לילדים
	yesh lakhem manot liyladim?

Can I have a highchair/ child's seat please?	כיסא אוכל לתינוק, בבקשה. *kise okhel latinok, bevakasha.*
Where can I feed/ change the baby?	איפה אוכל להאכיל/להחליף לתינוק? *eyfo ukhal leha-akhil/lehakhlif latinok?*
Can you warm this?	אתה יכול לחמם את זה? / את יכולה לחמם את זה? *ata yakhol lekhamem et ze?* **m** / *at yekhola lekhamem et ze?* **f**

For Traveling with Children, see page 148.

How to Complain

When will our food be ready?	מתי האוכל שלנו יהיה מוכן? *matay ha-okhel shelanu ihiye mukhan?*
We can't wait any longer.	אנחנו לא יכולים לחכות יותר. *anakhnu lo yekholim lekhakot yoter.*
We're leaving.	אנחנו עוזבים. *anakhnu ozvim.*
I didn't order this.	אני לא הזמנתי את זה. *ani lo hizmanti et ze.*
I ordered...	אני הזמנתי... *ani hizmanti...*
I can't eat this.	אני לא יכול לאכול את זה. / אני לא יכולה לאכול את זה. *ani lo yakhol le-ekhol et ze.* **m** / *ani lo yekhola le-ekhol et ze.* **f**

This is too...	...זה יותר מדי	ze yoter miday...
cold/hot	קר/חם	kar/kham
salty/spicy	מלוח/חריף	maluakh/kharif
tough/bland	קשה/בלי טעם	kashe/bli ta-am
This isn't clean/fresh.	זה לא נקי/טרי.	ze lo naki/tari.

Paying

The check [bill], please.	את החשבון, בבקשה.	et hakheshbon, bevakasha.
Separate checks [bills], please.	חשבונות נפרדים, בבקשה.	kheshbonot nifradim, bevakasha.
It's all together.	זה ביחד.	ze beyakhad.
Is service included?	זה כולל שירות?	ze kolel sherut?
What's this amount for?	על מה הסכום הזה?	al ma haskhum haze?
I didn't have that.	אני לא הזמנתי את זה	ani lo hizmanti et ze.
I had...	...הזמנתי	hizmanti...
Can I have a receipt/ an itemized bill?	אפשר לקבל קבלה/חשבון מפורט?	efshar lekabel kabala/kheshbon meforat?
That was delicious!	זה היה טעים!	ze haya ta-im!
I've already paid.	שילמתי כבה.	shilamti kvar.

Israel is a blend of international culinary cultures and as such, there are all types of foodie delights on the menu. Common spices include cumin, fresh and dried coriander, mint, garlic, onion, turmeric, black pepper, cardamom and fresh green chilli. Dark fruity olive oil adds further fragrance. Arab food is considered "Oriental" but both Arab and Jewish meals begin in a similar way – with many small dishes such as houmous, aubergine dips, pickled vegetables and salads.

Breakfast

butter	חמאה	khem-a
...coffee/tea	...קפה/תה	kafe/te...
black	שחור	shakhor
decaf	נטול קפאין	netul kafain
with milk	עם חלב	im khalav
with sugar	עם סוכר	im sukar
with artificial sweetener	עם ממתיק מלאכותי	im mamtik melakhuti
cold/hot cereal	דייסה קרה/חמה	daysa kara/khama
cold cuts	נקניקים	naknikim
croissant	קרואסון	kroason
jam/jelly	ריבה	riba
marmalade	מרמלדה	marmelada
cheese	גבינה	gvina
...juice	...מיץ	mitz...
Orange	תפוזים	tapuzim
Apple	תפוחים	tapukhim
Grapefruit	אשכוליות	eshkoliyot

milk	חלב *khalav*
oatmeal [porridge]	דייסת שיבולת שועל *daysat shibolet shual*
water	מים *ma-im*
granola [muesli]	גרנולה (מוזלי) *granola (muzli)*
muffin	מופין *mofin*
...egg	...ביצה *beytza...*
hard /soft-boiled	קשה/רכה *kasha/raka*
fried	עין *ayin*
scrambled	מקושקשת *mekushkeshet*
omelette	אומלט *omlet*
bread	לחם *lekhem*
toast	טוסט *tost*
roll	לחמניה *lakhmanya*
sausage	נקניקיה *naknikiya*
yogurt	יוגורט *yogurt*

Snack items such as sesame breads with za'atar, pizza, blintzes, waffles and burgers, not to mention falafel are a staple of the Israeli diet. All of these items can all be readily found on roadside stands and in stalls within the souks.

Appetizers

avocado	אבוקדו *avocado*
blintzes	בלינצ'ס *blinches*
chopped liver	כבד קצוץ *kaved katzutz*
hummous	חומוס *khumus*
latkes	לביבות *levivot*
melon	מלון *melon*

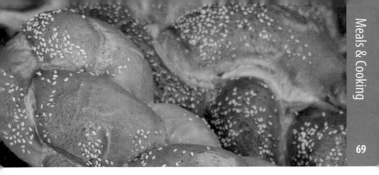

pancakes	פנקייק *pankeyk*
salad	סלט *salat*
shakshuka	שקשוקה *shakshuka*
tahini	טחינה *tkhina*

Soup

beef soup	מרק בקר *marak bakar*
borscht	בורשט *bursht*
chicken soup	מרק עוף *marak of*
chicken soup with dumplings	מרק עוף עם כופתאות *marak of im kufta-ot*
fish soup	מרק דגים *marak dagim*
fruit soup	מרק פירות *marak perot*
noodle soup	מרק אטריות *marak itriyot*
onion soup	מרק בצל *marak batzal*
potato soup	מרק תפוחי אדמה *marak tapukhey adama*
tomato soup	מרק עגבניות *marak agvanyot*
vegetable soup	מרק ירקות *marak yerakot*

Fish & Seafood

| carp | קרפיון *karpiyon* |
| clams | צדפות *tzdafot* |

cod	קוד *cod*
herring	הרינג *hering*
mullet	בורי *buri*
mussels	מולים *mulim*
octopus	תמנון *tamnun*
salmon	סלמון *salmon*
shrimp [prawns]	שרימפס [פראון] *shrimps*
sole	סול *sol*
sprats (small herring)	הרינג גמדי *hering gamadi*
St. Peter's fish	אמנון, מושט *thsum, nonma*
trout	פורל *forel*
tuna	טונה *tuna*

Meat & Poultry

beef	בשר בקר *besar bakar*
chicken	עוף *of*
chicken shashlik	שישליק עוף *shishlik of*
duck	ברווז *barvaz*
goose	אווז *avaz*
kebab	קבב *kabab*
lamb	טלה *tale*
partridge	חוגלה *khugla*
pheasant	פסיון *pasion*
quail	שליו *slav*
sausages	נקניקיות *naknikiyot*
steak	סטייק *steyk*
stew of meat & beans, traditionally eaten on the Sabbath	צלי של בשר ושעועית, בדרך כלל נאכל ביום שבת *tzli shel basar veshe-u-it, bederekh klal ne-ekhal beyom shabat*
turkey	תרנגול הודו *tarnegol hodu*
veal	עגל *egel*

Do not expect to find pork on offer in either a kosher or Muslim restaurant as both religions prohibit its consumption. Seafood, while forbidden by Jewish law and permissible by Muslim, is widely available. Fish is generally excellent. Most beef is imported but chicken and lamb are easy to come by.

Vegetables & Staples

cabbage	כרוב	*kruv*
carrots	גזר	*gezer*
celery	סלרי	*seleri*
cucumber	מלפפון	*melafefon*
eggplant [aubergine]	חציל	*khatzil*
garlic	שום	*shum*
green beans	שעועית ירוקה	*she-u-it yeruka*
lettuce	חסה	*khasa*
mushrooms	פטריות	*pitriyot*
onions	בצל	*batzal*
peas	אפונה	*afuna*
peppers (red, green)	פלפלים (אדום, ירוק)	*pilpelim (adom/yarok)*

potatoes	תפוחי אדמה	*tapukhey adama*
red cabbage	כרוב אדום	*kruv adom*
rice	אורז	*orez*
shallots [spring onions]	בצל ירוק	*batzal yarok*
rutabaga [swede]	לפת צהובה	*lefet tzehuba*
spinach	תרד	*tered*
tomatoes	עגבניות	*agvanyot*
zucchini [courgettes]	קישוא	*kishu*

Fruit

apples	תפוחי עץ	*tapukhey etz*
apricots	משמשים	*mishmeshim*
avocado	אבוקדו	*avocado*
bananas	בננות	*bananot*
barberries	ברבריס	*barbiris*
blackberries	פטל שחור	*petel shakhor*
blackcurrants	ענבי שועל	*anvey shual*
cherries	דובדבנים	*duvdevanim*
dates	תמרים	*tmarim*
figs	תאנים	*te-enim*

grapefruit	אשכוליות	*eshkoliyot*
grapes	ענבים	*anavim*
mandarins	מנדרינות	*manderinot*
mango	מנגו	*mango*
melon	מלונים	*melonim*
olives	זיתים	*zeytim*
oranges	תפוזים	*tapuzim*
peaches	אפרסקים	*afarsekim*
pears	אגסים	*agasim*
persimmon	אפרסמונים	*afarsemonim*
pineapple	אננס	*ananas*
plums	שזיפים	*shezifim*
pomegranates	רימונים	*rimonim*
raspberries	פטל אדום	*petel adom*
strawberries	תות שדה	*tut sade*
sultanas	סולטנה	*sultana*
tangerines	קלמנטינות	*klemantinot*
watermelon	אבטיח	*avati-akh*

Parve means a food that is neither meat nor dairy. While this includes fruit and vegetables, parve usually refers to an artificial milk substitute that can be eaten after meat, for instance, **parve** ice cream.

Dessert

apple cake	עוגת תפוחי עץ	*ugat tapukhey etz*
apple strudel	שטרודל תפוחי עץ	*shtrudel tapukhey etz*
baklava	בקלאווה	*baklava*
cheesecake	עוגת גבינה	*ugat gvina*
crème caramel	קרם קרמל	*krem karamel*
custard pudding	רפרפת	*rafrefet*
chocolate pudding	פודינג שוקולד	*puding shokolad*
fruit compote	לפתן פירות	*liftan perot*
frozen yoghurt	יוגורט קפוא	*yogurt kafu*
icecream	גלידה	*glida*
New Year's honey cake	עוגת דבש לראש השנה	*ugat dvash lerosh hashana*
pancakes	פנקייק	*pankeyk*
poppy seed cake	עוגת פרג	*ugat pereg*

Sauces & Condiments

ketchup	קטשופ	*ketshop*
mustard	חרדל	*khardal*
pepper	פלפל	*pilpel*
salt	מלח	*melakh*

At the Market

Where are the trolleys/baskets?	איפה העגלות/סלסלות? *eyfo ha-agalot/salsalot?*
Where is...?	איפה...? *eyfo...?*
I'd like some of that/this.	אני רוצֶה קצת מזה. / אני רוצָה קצת מזה. *ani rotze ktzat mize. m / ani rotza ktzat mize. f*
Can I taste it?	אפשר לטעום? *efshar lit-om?*
I'd like...	אני רוצֶה... / אני רוצָה... *ani rotze... m / ani rotza... f*
a kilo/half kilo of...	קילו/חצי קילו... *kilo/khetzi kilo...*
a liter of...	ליטר... *liter...*
a piece of...	חתיכה של... *khatikha shel...*
a slice of...	נתח... *netakh...*
More./Less.	יותר./פחות. *yoter./pakhot.*
How much?	כמה זה עולה? *kama ze ole?*
Where do I pay?	איפה משלמים? *eyfo meshalmim?*
A bag, please.	שקית, בבקשה. *sakit, bevakasha.*
I'm being helped.	כבר עוזרים לי. *kvar ozrim li.*

For Conversion Tables, see page 179.

In the Kitchen

bottle opener	פותחן בקבוקים
	potkhan bakbukim
bowl	קערה *ke-ara*
can opener	פותחן קופסת שימורים
	potkhan kufsat shimurim
corkscrew	חולץ פקקים *kholetz pkakim*
cup	ספל *sefel*
fork	מזלג *mazleg*
frying pan	מחבת לטיגון
	makhvat letigun
glass	כוס *kos*
(steak) knife	סכין (סטייק) *sakin (steyk)*
measuring	כוס/כף מדידה
cup/spoon	*kos/kaf medida*
napkin	מפית *mapit*
plate	צלחת *tzalakhat*
pot	סיר *sir*
spatula	מרית *marit*
spoon	כף *kaf*

YOU MAY HEAR...

אפשר לעזור? *efshar la-azor?*	Can I help you?
מה תרצה? / מה תרצי? *ma tirtze?* **m** / *ma tirzi?* **f**	What would you like?
עוד משהו? *od mashehu?*	Anything else?
זה...שקל. *ze... shekel.*	That's...shekel.

Measurements in Israel are metric and that applies to the weight of food too. If you tend to think in pounds and ounces, it's worth brushing up on what the metric equivalent is before you go shopping for fruit and veg in markets and supermarkets. Five hundred grams, or half a kilo, is a common quantity to order, and that converts to just over a pound (17.65 ounces, to be precise).

YOU MAY SEE...

מומלץ עד תאריך...	best if used by...
קלוריות	calories
ללא שומן	fat free
לשמור בקירור	keep refrigerated
עשוי להכיל עקבות של...	may contain traces of...
ניתן לחמם במיקרוגל	microwaveable
למכירה עד...	sell by...
מתאים לצמחונים	suitable for vegetarians

Drinks

ESSENTIAL

The wine list/drink menu, please.	רשימת היינות/תפריט המשקאות, בבקשה. *reshimat hayeynot/tafrit hamashka-ot, bevakasha.*
What do you recommend?	?על מה אתה ממליץ / על מה את ממליצה *al ma ata mamlitz? m / al ma at mamlitza? f*
I'd like a bottle/glass of red/white wine.	אני רוצֶה בקבוק/כוס יין אדום/לבן. אני רוצָה בקבוק/כוס יין אדום/לבן. *ani rotze bakbuk/kos ya-in adom/lavan. m* *ani rotza bakbuk/kos yain adom/lavan. f*
The house wine, please.	היין של הבית, בבקשה. *haya-in shel habait, bevakasha.*
Another bottle/glass, please.	עוד בקבוק/כוס, בבקשה. *od bakbuk/kos, bevakasha.*
I'd like a local beer.	אני רוצֶה בירה מקומית. / אני רוצָה בירה מקומית. *ani rotze bira mekomit. m / ani rotza bira mekomit. f*
Can I buy you a drink?	?אפשר לקנות לְךָ משקה? / אפשר לקנות לָךְ משקה *efshar liknot lekha mashke? m /* *efshar liknot lakh mashke? f*
Cheers!	!לחיים *lekha-im!*
A coffee/tea, please.	קפה/תה בבקשה. *kafe/te bevakasha.*
Black.	שחור. *shakhor.*
With...	...עם *im...*
milk	חלב *khalav*
sugar	סוכר *sukar*
artificial sweetener	ממתיק מלאכותי *mamtik melakhuti*
A..., please.	..., בבקשה. *..., bevakasha.*
juice	מיץ *mitz*

| soda | זגומ הקשמ *mashke mugaz* |
| (sparkling/still) water | מים (סילרנימ/הדוס) *ma-im (soda/mineralim)* |

Non-alcoholic Drinks

coffee	קפה *kafe*
hot chocolate	שוקולטה *shokolata*
juice	מיץ *mitz*
lemonade	לימונדה *limonada*
milk	חלב *khalav*
soda	משקה מוגז *mashke mugaz*
(iced) tea	תה (קר) *te (kar)*
(sparkling/still) water	מים (סודה/מינרלים) *ma-im (soda/mineralim)*

The café culture is massive in Israel and it is not uncommon to spend hours with friends at a streetside café over coffee and cake. Tea on the other hand is not as popular and the selection available may be disappointing. Fruit juices are greatly popular too. Note that as in Britain, soda refers to soda water and not soft drinks as in the US.

YOU MAY HEAR...

את רוצה לשתות משהו? אתה רוצה לשתות משהו? *ata rotze lishtot mashehu?* **m**/ *at rotza lishtot mashehu?* **f**	Can I get you a drink?
עם חלב או סוכר? *im khalav o sukar?* סילרנימ סימ וא הדוס? *soda o ma-im mineralim?*	With milk or sugar? Sparkling or still water?

Apéritifs, Cocktails & Liqueurs

arak	עראק *arak*
brandy	בראנדי *brandi*
gin	ג'ין *jin*
rum	רום *rum*
scotch	סקוטש *skotsh*
tequila	הליקט *tekila*
vodka	וודקה *vodka*
whisky	וויסקי *viski*

Beer

...beer	...בירה *bira...*
bottled/draft	בבקבוק/מחבית *bebakbuk/mehakhavit*
dark/light	כהה/בהירה *keha/behira*

The local speciality is arak, which is similar to Greece's ouzo.

lager/pilsener	לאגר/פילזנר	*lager/pilsner*
local/imported	מקומית/מיובאת	*mekomit/meyuvet*
non-alcoholic	לא-אלכוהולית	*lo-alkoholit*

Wine

. . . wine	. . . יין	*ya-in . . .*
red/white	אדום/לבן	*adom/lavan*
house/table	בית/שולחן	*ba it/shulkhan*
dry/sweet	יבש/מתוק	*yavesh/matok*
sparkling	תוסס	*toses*
champagne	שמפניה	*shampanya*
dessert wine	יין קינוח	*yen kinu-akh*

All restaurants and cafés serve alcohol and there is a wide
selection of local and imported wines and beer and spirits
available. That said, most Israeli Jews consume relatively small
amounts of alcohol compared to Europeans and Americans. Heavy
drinking and smelling of alcohol is badly viewed — drinking 4 to 5
beers a day may be considered excessive.

On the Menu

cilantro [coriander]	זרעי כוסברה	*zirey kusbara*
almond	שקד	*shaked*
anchovy	אנשובי	*enshobi*
apple	תפוח עץ	*tapuakh etz*
apricot	משמש	*mishmesh*
artichoke	ארטישוק	*artishok*
artificial sweetener	ממתיק מלאכותי	*mamtik melakhuti*
asparagus	אספרגוס	*asparagos*
avocado	אבוקדו	*avokad*
bacon	בייקון	*beykon*
banana	בננה	*banana*
barberries	ברבריס	*barbiris*
basil	בזיליקום	*bazilikum*
bass	סב	*bas*
bay leaf	עלה דפנה	*ale dafna*
bean sprouts	נבטי שעועית	*nivtey sheuit*
beans	שעועית	*she-u-it*
beef	בשר בקר	*besar bakar*
beer	בירה	*bira*
beet	סלק	*selek*
black pepper	פלפל שחור	*pilpel shakhor*
blackberry	פטל שחור	*petel shakhor*
blackcurrants	ענבי שועל	*anvey shu-al*
blood sausage	נקניקיית דם	*naknikiyat dam*
blue cheese	גבינה כחולה	*gvina kkhula*
blueberry	אוכמניות	*ukhmaniyot*
brandy	ברנדי	*brandi*
bread	לחם	*lekhem*
breast (of chicken)	חזה (עוף)	*khaze (of)*

broth	מרק בשר	*marak bashar*
Brussels sprouts	כרוב ניצנים	*kruv nitzanim*
butter	חמאה	*khem-a*
buttermilk	לבן	*leben*
butternut squash	דלורית	*dalorit*
cabbage	כרוב	*kruv*
cake	עוגה	*uga*
candy [sweets]	ממתקים	*mamtakim*
caper	צלף	*tzalaf*
capers	צלפים	*tzalafim*
caramel	קרמל	*karamel*
caraway	קימל	*kimel*
carrot	גזר	*gezer*
cashew	קשיו	*kashyu*
cauliflower	כרובית	*kruvit*
celery	סלרי	*seleri*
cereal	דייסה	*daysa*
cheese	גבינה	*gvina*
cherry	דובדבן	*duvdevan*
chestnut	ערמון	*armon*
chicken	עוף	*of*

chickpeas	גרגרי חומוס *gargerey khumus*
chicory, endive	עולש *olesh*
chili pepper	פלפל צ׳ילי *pilpel chili*
chives	עירית *irit*
chocolate	שוקולד *shokolad*
chop	צלע *tzela*
cider	סיידר *sayder*
cinnamon	קינמון *kinamon*
clams	צדפות *tzdafot*
clove	ציפורן *tziporen*
coconut	קוקוס *kokus*
cod	קוד *kod*
coffee	קפה *kafe*
cold cuts	נקניקים *naknikim*
cookie [biscuit]	עוגיה *ugiya*
crab	סרטן *sartan*
crabmeat	בשר סרטן *besar sartan*
cracker	קרקר *kreker*
cranberry	חמוצית *khamutzit*
crayfish	סרטן הנהרות *sartan haneharot*
cream	שמנת *shamenet*

cream, whipped	קצפת	katzefet
croissant	קרואסון	kroason
cucumber	מלפפון	melafefon
cumin	כמון	kamun
custard	רפרפת	rafrefet
date	תמר	tamar
dessert wine	יין קינוח	yen kinuakh
dill	שמיר	shamir
duck	ברווז	barvaz
eel	צלופח	tzlophakh
egg	ביצה	beytza
egg yolk/white	חלבון/חלמון	khelbon/khelmon
eggplant [aubergine]	חציל	khatzil
falafel	פָלָאפֶל	falafel
fennel	שומר	shumar
fig	תאנה	te-ena
fish	דג	dag
French fries	צ׳יפס	chips
fritter	פריטר	friter
fruit	פירות	perot
game	בשר ציד	besar tzaid

garlic	שום	*shum*
garlic sauce	רוטב שום	*rotev shum*
gefilte fish	גפילטע פיש	*gefilte fish*
gherkin/pickle	מלפפון חמוץ	*melafefon khamutz*
giblets	קורקבנים	*kurkevanim*
gin	ג'ין	*jin*
ginger	זנגביל	*zangevil*
goat	עז	*ez*
goose	אווז	*avaz*
grape	ענב	*enav*
grapefruit	אשכולית	*eshkolit*
green beans	שעועית ירוקה	*she-u-it yeruka*
guava	גויאבה	*guyava*
guinea fowl	עוף גינאי	*of gine-i*
haddock	חמור ים	*khamor yam*
hake	בקלה	*bakala*
halibut	הליבוט	*hallibut*
ham	ירך חזיר	*yarekh khazir*
hamburger	המבורגר	*hamburger*
hazelnut	אגוזי לוז	*egozey luz*
heart	לב	*lev*

heavy cream	שמנת מתוקה	*shamenet metuka*
hen	תרנגולת	*tarnegolet*
herbs	עשבי תיבול	*isvey tibul*
herring	הרינג	*hering*
honey	דבש	*dvash*
hot dog	נקניקיה	*naknikiya*
hot pepper sauce	רוטב פלפל חריף	*rotev pilpel kharif*
ice (cube)	קרח (קוביות)	*kerakh (kubiyot)*
ice cream	גלידה	*glida*
jam	ריבה	*riba*
jelly	ג'לי	*jeli*
juice	מיץ	*mitz*
ketchup	קטשופ	*ketshop*
kid (young goat)	גדי	*gdi*
kidney	כליה	*kilya*
kiwi	קיוי	*kivi*
knish	קנישס	*kenishes*
lamb	טלה	*tale*
leek	כרשה	*kresha*
leg	רגל	*regel*
lemon	לימון	*limon*

lemon soda	סודה לימון	*soda limon*
lentils	עדשים	*adashim*
lettuce	חסה	*khasa*
lime	חושחש	*khushkhash*
liqueur	ליקר	*liker*
liver	כבד	*kaved*
lobster	לובסטר	*lobster*
loin	מותן	*moten*
macaroni	מקרוני	*makaroni*
mackerel	מקרל	*makarel*
mango	מנגו	*mango*
margarine	מרגרינה	*margarina*
marmalade	מרמלדה	*marmelada*
marzipan	מרציפן	*martzipan*
Matzo balls	קניידלך	*kneydalekh*
mayonnaise	מיונז	*mayonez*
meat	בשר	*basar*
meatballs	קציצות	*ktzitzot*
melon	מלון	*melon*
meringue	מרנג	*mareng*
milk	חלב	*khalav*

mint	נענע	*nana*
monkfish	מלאך ים כנוף	*malakh yam kanuf*
mushroom	פטריה	*pitriya*
mussels	מולים	*mulim*
mustard	חרדל	*khardal*
mutton	בשר כבש	*basar keves*
noodle	אטריה	*itriya*
nutmeg	אגוז מוסקט	*egoz muskat*
nuts	אגוזים	*egozim*
octopus	תמנון	*tamnun*
okra	במיה	*bamiya*
olive	זית	*za-it*
olive oil	שמן זית	*shemen za-it*
omelet	אומלט	*omlet*
onion	בצל	*batzal*
orange	תפוז	*tapuz*
orange liqueur	ליקר תפוזים	*liker tapuzim*
orange soda [squash]	סודה תפוז	*soda tapuz*
oregano	אורגנו	*oregano*
organ meat [offal]	בשר אברים פנימיים	*besar evarim pnimiyim*
ox tail	זנב שור	*znav shor*

oyster	צדפה *tz-dafa*
pancake	פנקייק *pankeyke*
papaya	פפאיה *papaya*
parsley	פטרוזיליה *petruzilya*
parsnip	גזר לבן *gezer lavan*
pasta	פסטה *pasta*
pastries	מאפים *ma-afim*
pâté	פטה *pate*
peach	אפרסק *afarsek*
peanut	בוטן *boten*
pear	אגס *agas*
peas	אפונה *afuna*
pecan	פקאן *pekan*
pepper (vegetable)	פלפל *pilpel*
pheasant	פסיון *pasion*
pie	פאי *pay*
pineapple	אננס *ananas*
pizza	פיצה *pitza*
plum	שזיף *shazif*
pomegranate	רימון *rimon*
port	פורט *port*

potato	תפוח אדמה *tapuakh adama*
potato chips [crisps]	צ'יפס תפוחי אדמה *chips (tapukhey adama)*
poultry	בשר עוף *besar of*
prune	שזיף מיובש *shazif meyubash*
pumpkin	דלעת *dla-at*
quail	שליו *slav*
rabbit	ארנבת *arnevet*
radish	צנונית *tznonit*
raisin	צימוק *tzimuk*
raspberry	פטל אדום *petel adom*
red cabbage	כרוב אדום *kruv adom*
red currant	דומדמנית *dumdemanit*
rhubarb	ריבס *ribas*
rice	אורז *orez*
roast	צלי *tzli*
roast beef	צלי בשר בקר *tzli besar bakar*
roll	לחמניה *lakhmanya*
rosemary	רוזמרין *rozmarin*
rum	רום *rum*
saffron	זעפרן *za-afran*
sage	מרוה *marva*

salad	סלט	*salat*
salami	סלמי	*salami*
salmon	אלתית	*iltit*
salmon	סלמון	*salmon*
salt	מלח	*melakh*
sandwich	כריך	*karikh*
sardine	סרדין	*sardin*
sauce	רוטב	*rotev*
sausage	נקניק	*naknik*
scallion [spring onion]	בצל ירוק	*batzal yarok*
scallops	סקלופס	*skalops*
scotch	סקוטש	*skotsh*
sea bass	לברק	*lavrak*
sea perch	נסיכת הנילוס	*nesikhat hanilus*
seafood	פירות ים	*perot yam*
shallot	בצלצל	*betzaltzal*
shark	כריש	*karish*
shellfish	רכיכות	*rekikhot*
sherry	שרי	*sheri*
shoulder	כתף	*katef*
shrimp/prawn	שרימפס/פראון	*shrimps/praun*

sirloin	סינטה *sinata*
snack	חטיף *khatif*
snail	חילזון *khilazon*
soda	משקה מוגז *mashke mugaz*
soft, creamy cheese	גבינה למריחה, רכה *gvina levana, raka*
soft, new cheese	גבינה רכה, טריה *gvina raka, triya*
sole	סול *sol*
soup	מרק *marak*
sour cream	שמנת חמוצה *shamenet khamutza*
soy sauce	רוטב סויה *rotev soya*
soya /soybean [soya bean]	סויה/פולי סויה *soya/poley soya*
soya milk	חלב סויה *khalav soya*
spaghetti	ספגטי *spageti*
spices	תבלינים *tavlinim*
spinach	תרד *tered*
spirits	ספירט *spirt*
squid	דיונון *diyonun*
St. Peter's fish	אמנון, מושט *amnon, musht*
steak	סטייק *steyk*
stew	נזיד *nazid*

stewed fruit	פירות מאודים *perot me-udim*
strawberry	תות שדה *tut sade*
sugar	סוכר *sukar*
sweet and sour sauce	רוטב חמוץ מתוק *rotev khamutz matok*
sweet corn	תירס מתוק *tiras matok*
sweet pepper	פלפל מתוק, פפריקה *pilpel matok, paprika*
sweet potato	תפוח אדמה מתוק *tapuakh adama matok*
swordfish	דג חרב *dag kherev*
syrup	סירופ *sirop*
tangerine	קלמנטינה *klementina*
tarragon	טרגון *taragon*
tea	תה *te*
thyme	תימין *timin*
toast	טוסט *tost*
tofu	טופו *tofu*
tomato	עגבניה *agvaniya*
tongue	לשון *lashon*
tonic water	מי טוניק *mey tonik*
tripe	קיבה *keyva*
trout	פורל *forel*
truffle	פטריות כמהין *pitriyot kamehin*

tuna	טונה	*tuna*
turkey	תרנגול הודו	*tarnegol hodu*
turnip	לפת	*lefet*
vanilla	וניל	*vanil*
veal	עגל	*egel*
vegetables	ירקות	*yerakot*
venison	בשר צבי	*besar tzvi*
vermouth	ורמוט	*vermot*
vinegar	חומץ	*khometz*
vodka	וודקה	*vodka*
waffle	ופל	*vafel*
water	מים	*ma-im*
watercress	גרגיר הנחלים	*gargir hanekhalim*
watermelon	אבטיח	*avati-akh*
wheat	חיטה	*khita*
whisky	ויסקי	*viski*
wine	יין	*yain*
yogurt	יוגורט	*yogurt*
zucchini [courgette]	קישוא	*kishu*

People

ESSENTIAL

Hello./Hi!	שלום!/היי! *shalom/hay!*
How are you?	מה שלומך? / מה שלומך? *ma shlomkha? **m** / ma shlomekh? **f***
Fine, thanks.	טוב, תודה. *tov, toda.*
Excuse me [sorry]!	סליחה! *slikha!*
Do you speak English?	האם אתה מדבר אנגלית?/ האם את מדברת אנגלית? *ha-im ata medaber anglit? **m** / ha-im at medaberet anglit? **f***
What's your name?	איך קוראים לך? / איך קוראים לך? *eykh korim lekha? **m** / eykh korim lakh? **f***
My name is...	קוראים לי... *korim li...*
Nice to meet you.	נעים להכיר. *na-im lehakir.*
Where are you from?	מאיפה אתה? / מאיפה את? *me-eyfo ata? **m** / me-eyfo at? **f***
I'm from the U.K./U.S.	אני מאנגליה/מארצות הברית. *ani me-angliya/me-artzot habrit.*
What do you do for a living?	מה אתה עושה בחיים? / מה את עושה בחיים? *ma ata ose bakhayim? **m** / ma at osa bakhayim? **f***
I work for...	אני עובד עבור... / אני עובדת עבור... *ani oved avur... **m** / ani ovedet avur... **f***
I'm a student.	אני סטודנט. / אני סטודנטית. *ani student **m** / ani studentit **f***
I'm retired.	אני גמלאי. / אני גמלאית. *ani gimla-i **m** /ani gimla-it **f***
Do you like...?	אתה אוהב...? / את אוהבת...? *ata ohev...? **m** / at ohevet...? **f***
Goodbye.	שלום /ביי. *shalom /bie.*
See you later.	להתראות. *lehitraot.*

As a result of the massive wave of immigration from Russia since the 90's, cyrillic shop signs abound, vying for space among the Hebrew, English and Arabic lettering. Newstands are also bursting with Russian-language publications and in some suburbs of Tel Aviv, Russian is the lingua franca. While this may at first be confusing at first, it is just another element of the mix of cultures in Israel.

Language Difficulties

Do you speak English?	האם אתה מדבר אנגלית? / האם את מדברת אנגלית?
	ha-im ata medaber anglit? m /
	ha-im at medaberet anglit? f
Does anyone here speak English?	יש כאן מישהו שמדבר אנגלית?
	yesh kan mishehu shemedaber anglit?
I don't speak (much) Hebrew.	אני לא מדבר (הרבה) עברית.
	אני לא מדברת (הרבה) עברית.
	ani lo medaber (harbe) ivrit m/
	ani lo medaberet (harbe) ivrit. f
Can you speak more slowly?	אפשר לדבר יותר לאט?
	efshar ledaber yoter le-at?
Can you repeat that?	אפשר לחזור על זה? *efshar lakhazor al ze?*
Excuse me?/ Sorry?	סליחה? *slikha?*
Can you spell it?	הז תא תייאל רשפא? *efshar le-ayet at ze?*
Please write it down.	תכתוב את זה בבקשה. / תכתבי את זה בבקשה.
	tikhtov et ze bevakasha. m / tikhtevi et ze bevakasha. f
Can you translate this into English for me?	אתה יכול לתרגם את זה לאנגלית בשבילי?
	את יכולה לתרגם את זה לאנגלית בשבילי?
	ata yakhol letargem et ze le-anglit bishvili? m /
	at yekhola letargem et ze le-anglit bishvili? f

YOU MAY HEAR...

אני מדבר רק קצת אנגלית. / אני מדברת רק קצת אנגלית. *ani medaber rak ktzat anglit.* **m** / *ani medaberet rak ktzat anglit.* **f**	I only speak a little English.
אני לא מדבר אנגלית. /אני לא מדברת אנגלית. *ani lo medaber anglit.* **m** /*ani lo medaberet anglit.* **f**	I don't speak English.

What does this/ that mean?	מה זה אומר? *ma ze omer?*	
I understand.	אני מבין. / אני מבינה. *ani mevin.* **m** / *ani mevina.* **f**	
I don't understand.	אני לא מבין. / אני לא מבינה. *ani lo mevin.* **m** / *ani lo mevina.* **f**	
Do you understand?	אתה מבין? / את מבינה? *ata mevin?* **m** / *at mevina?* **f**	

Making Friends

Hello!	שלום! *shalom!*
Good afternoon.	אחר צהרים טובים. *akhar tzohora-im tovim.*
Good evening.	ערב טוב. *erev-tov*

My name is...	...קוראים ל *korim li...*
What's your name?	איך קוראים לךָ? / איך קוראים לךְ? *eykh korim lekha? m / eykh korim lakh? f*
I'd like to introduce you to...	...אני רוצֶה להכיר אותךָ ל / ...אני רוצָה להכיר אותךְ ל *ani rotze m lehakir otkha m le... / ani rotza f lehakir otakh f le...*
Pleased to meet you.	נעים להכיר. *na-im lehakir.*
How are you?	מה שלומךָ? / מה שלומךְ? *ma shlomkha? m / ma shlomekh? f*
Fine, thanks. And you?	טוב, תודה. ואתה? / טוב, תודה. ואתְ? *tov, toda. Ve-ata? m / tov, toda. Ve-at? f*

Many slang words have worked their way into the Hebrew language such as **svetcher** for sweatshirt and **sveder** for sweater and even **breks** for brakes! Most of these words have Hebrew equivalents, which have been pushed aside in common usage.

Travel Talk

I'm here...	...אני כאן *ani kan*...
on business	בעסקים *be-asakim*
on vacation [holiday]	בחופשה *bekhufsha*
studying	בלימודים *belimudim*
I'm staying for...	אני נשאר *ani nishar*
I've been here...	...אני כאן כבר *ani kan kvar*...
a day	יום *yom*
a week	שבוע *shavu-a*
a month	חודש *khodesh*
Where are you from?	?מאיפה אתה? / מאיפה את
	me-eyfo ata? **m** / *me-eyfo at?* **f**
I'm from...	...אני מ *ani me*...

For Numbers, see page 174.

Personal

Who are you with?	?עם מי אתה כאן? / עם מי את כאן
	im mi ata kan? **m** / *im mi at kan?* **f**
I'm here alone.	אני כאן לבד. *ani kan levad.*
I'm with...	...אני עם *ani im*...
my husband/wife	בעלי/אשתי *ba-ali/ishti*
my boyfriend/	החבר/החברה שלי
girlfriend	*hakhaver/hakhavera sheli*
a friend	חבר / חברה *khaver* **m** / *khavera* **f**
friends	חברים *khaverim*
a colleague	עמית / עמיתה *amit* **m** / *amita* **f**
colleagues	עמיתים *amitim*
When's your birthday?	?מתי יום ההולדת שלך? / מתי יום ההולדת שלך
	matay yom hahuledet shelkha? **m** /
	matay yom hahuledet shelakh? **f**

How old are you?	‫בן כמה אתה? / בת כמה את?‬
	ben kama ata? **m** / *bat kama at?* **f**
I'm...	‫אני בן... / אני בת...‬ *ani ben...* **m** / *ani bat...* **f**
Are you married?	‫אתה נשוי? / את נשואה?‬
	ata nasuy? **m** / *at nesu-a?* **f**
I'm...	‫אני...‬ *ani...*
single	‫רווק / רווקה‬ *ravak* **m** / *ravaka* **f**
in a relationship	‫במערכת יחסים‬ *bema-arekhet yakhasim*
engaged	‫מאורס / מאורסת‬ *me-oras* **m** / *me-oreset* **f**
married	‫נשוי / נשואה‬ *nasuy* **m** / *nesu-a* **f**
divorced	‫גרוש / גרושה‬ *garush* **m** / *grusha* **f**
separated	‫פרוד / פרודה‬ *parud* **m** / *pruda* **f**
widowed	‫אלמן / אלמנה‬ *alman* **m** / *almana* **f**
Do you have children/ grandchildren?	‫יש לך ילדים/ נכדים? / יש לך ילדים?‬ *yesh lekha yeladim/nekhadim?* **m** / *yesh lakh yeladim/nekhadim?* **f**

For Numbers, see page 174.

Work & School

What do you do for a living?	‫מה את עושה בחיים? / מה אתה עושה בחיים?‬ *ma ata ose bakhayim?* **m** / *ma at osa bakhayim?* **f**

What are you studying?	מה אתה לומד? / מה את לומדת?
	ma ata lomed? **m** / *ma at lomedet?* **f**
I'm studying Hebrew.	אני לומד עברית. / אני לומדת עברית.
	ani lomed ivrit. **m** / *ani lomedet ivrit.* **f**
I...	נא... *ani...*
work full-/part-time	עובד / עובדת במשרה מלאה/חלקית
	oved **m** / *ovedet* **f** *bemisra mele-a/khelkit*
am unemployed	מובטל / מובטלת
	muvtal **m** / *muvtelet* **f**
work at home	עובד מהבית / עובדת מהבית
	oved mehaba-it **m** / *ovedet mehaba-it* **f**
Who do you work for?	בשביל מי אתה עובד? / בשביל מי את עובדת?
	bishvil mi ata oved? **m** / *bishvil mi at ovedet?* **f**
I work for...	אני עובד עבור... / אני עובדת עבור...
	ani oved avur... **m** / *ani ovedet avur...* **f**
Here's my business card.	הנה כרטיס הביקור שלי.
	hine kartis habikur sheli.

For Business Travel, see page 145.

Weather

What's the forecast?	מה תחזית מזג האוויר? *ma takhazit mezeg ha-avir?*
What beautiful/terrible weather!	איזה מזג אוויר יפה/ נוראי !
	eyze mezeg avir yafe/nora-i!
It's...	היום... *hayom...*
cool/warm	קריר/חמים *karir/khamim*
cold/hot	קר/חם *kar/kham*
rainy/sunny	גשום/שמשי *gashum/shimshi*
snowy/icy	מושלג/קפוא *mushlag/kafu*
Do I need a jacket/an umbrella?	צריך לקחת מעיל/מטרייה?
	tzarikh lakakhat me-il/mitriya?

For Temperature, see page 180.

Romance

ESSENTIAL

Would you like to go out for a drink/dinner?	?אתה רוצה / את רוצה לצאת לשתות/לארוחת ערב *ata rotze* **m** */ at rotza* **f** *latzet lishtot/le-arukhat erev?*
What are your plans for tonight/ tomorrow?	?מה התוכניות שלך / שלך להלילה/ למחר *ma hatokhniyot shelkha* **m** */shelakh* **f** *lehalayla / lemakhar?*
Can I have your (phone) number?	?אפשר לקבל את המספר (טלפון) שלך / שלך *efshar lekabel et hamispar (telefon) shelkha* **m**/ *shelakh* **f**?
Can I join you?	?אפשר להצטרף אליך / אפשר להצטרף אלייך *efshar lehitztaref eleykha?* **m** / *efshar lehitztaref elayikh?* **f**
Can I buy you a drink?	?אפשר לקנות לך / לך משקה *efshar liknot lekha* **m** */lakh* **f** *mashke?*
I love you.	.אני אוהב אותך / אני אוהבת אותך *ani ohev* **m** *otakh* **f**. */ ani ohevet* **f** *otkha* **m**.

The Dating Game

Would you like to go out...?	?...אתה רוצה לצאת / את רוצה לצאת *ata rotze latzet...* **m** */ at rotza latzet...* **f**
for coffee	לקפה *lekafe*
for a drink	לשתות משהו *lishtot mashehu*
to dinner	לארוחת ערב *le-arukhat erev*

104

What are your plans for...?	?...מה התוכניות שלך ל / ?...מה התוכניות שלך ל *ma hatokhniyot shelkha **m** le...? /* *ma hatokhniyot shelakh **f** le...?*
today	היום *hayom*
tonight	הלילה *halayla*
tomorrow	מחר *makhar*
this weekend	סוף השבוע הזה *sof hashavu-a haze*
Where would you like to go?	?אן תרצה ללכת? / לאן תרצי ללכת *le-an tirtze lalekhet? **m** / le-an tirtzi lalekhet? **f***
I'd like to go to...	...רוצה ללכת ל / ...אני רוצה ללכת ל *ani rotze lalekhet le... **m** / ani rotza lalekhet le... **f***
Do you like...?	?...תה אוהב? / את אוהבת *ata ohev...? **m** / at ohevet...? **f***
Can I have your phone number/ email?	?אפשר לקבל את מספר הטלפון\אמייל שלך ?אפשר לקבל את מספר הטלפון\אמייל שלך *efshar lekabel et mispar hatelefon/haemail shelkha? **m*** *efshar lekabel et mispar hatelefon/haemail shelakh? **f***
Are you on Facebook /Twitter?	?אתה בפייסבוק/טוויטר? / את בפייסבוק/טוויטר *ata befeysbuk/twiter? **m** / at befeysbuk/twiter? **f***

Can I join you?	?אפשר להצטרף אליך / ?אפשר להצטרף אליך
	efshar lehitztaref eleykha? **m** / efshar lehitztaref elayikh? **f**
You're very attractive.	.אתה מאוד מושך / .את מאוד מושכת
	ata me-od moshekh. **m** / at me-od moshekhet. **f**
Let's go somewhere quieter.	.בוא נלך למקום שקט יותר / .בואי נלך למקום שקט יותר
	bo nelekh lemakom shaket yoter. **m** / bo-i nelekh lemakom shaket yoter. **f**

For Communications, see page 48.

Accepting & Rejecting

I'd love to.	.בשמחה
	besimkha.
Where should we meet?	?איפה ניפגש
	eyfo nipagesh?
I'll meet you at the bar/your hotel.	./אני אפגוש אותך בבר/במלון שלך
	.אני אפגוש אותך בבר/במלון שלך
	ani efgosh otakh babar/bamalon shelakh. **f** / ani efgosh otkha babar/bamalon shelakh. **m**
I'll come by at...	אני אבוא בשעה.... ani Avo Besha-a...
I'm busy.	.אני עסוק / .אני עסוקה ani asuk. **m** / ani asuka. **f**
I'm not interested.	.אני לא מעוניין / .אני לא מעוניינת
	ani lo me-unyan. **m** / ani lo me-unyenet. **f**
Leave me alone.	תעזוב אותי / תעזבי אותי
	ta-azov oti. **m** / ta-azvi oti. **f**
Stop bothering me!	!תפסיק להציק לי / !תפסיקי להציק לי
	tafsik lehatzik li! **m** / tafsiki lehatzik li! **f**

For Time, see page 176.

Israelis are quite informal and do not take offence if people are curt, likewise, you should not be offended if Israelis are curt with you.

Getting Intimate

Can I hug/kiss you?	?אני יכול לחבק/לנשק אותך
	?אני יכולה לחבק/לנשק אותך
	*ani yakhol **m** lekhabek/lenashek otakh **f**? /*
	*ani yekhola **f** lekhabek/lenashek otkha **m**?*
Yes.	כן. *ken.*
No.	לא. *lo.*
Stop!	תפסיק! / תפסיקי! *tafsik! **m** / tafsiki! **f***
I love you.	אני אוהב אותך./ אני אוהבת אותך.
	*ani ohev **m** otakh **f**./ ani ohevet **f** otkha **m**.*

Sexual Preferences

Are you gay?	?אתה עליז? / את עליזה *ata aliz? **m** / at aliza? **f***
I'm...	אני... *ani...*
heterosexual	הטרוסקסואלי/ אני הטרוסקסואלית
	*hetroseksu-ali **m** / hetroseksu-alit **f***
homosexual	הומו / לסבית *homo **m** / lesbit **f***
bisexual	דו מיני / דו מינית *du mini **m** / du minit **f***
Do you like men/	?אתה אוהב גברים/נשים
women?	?את אוהבת גברים/נשים
	*ata ohev **m** gvarim/nashim?*
	*at ohevet **f** gvarim/nashim?*

Leisure Time

Sightseeing

ESSENTIAL

Where's the tourist information office?	?המידע לתייר *eyfo misrad hameyda latayar?*
What are the main sights?	?הם אתרי התיירות העיקריים *mahem atarey hatayarut ha-ikariyim?*
Do you offer tours in English?	?אתם מציעים טיולים באנגלית *atem matzi-im tiyulim be-anglit?*
Can I have a map/guide?	?אפשר לקבל מפה/מדריך *efshar lekabel mapa/madrikh?*

Tourist Information

Do you have information on...?	?...יש לכם מידע על *yesh lakhem meyda al...?*
Can you recommend...?	?...אפשר לקבל המלצה לגבי *efshar lekabel hamlatza legabey...?*
a bus tour	אוטובוס טיולים *otobus tiyulim*
an excursion to...	...סיור ל *siyur le...*
a tour of...	...טיול ב *tiyul be...*

Tourists staying in Tel Aviv are entitled to three free English-language guided walking tours. Ask at a local tourist office for details.

On Tour

I'd like to go on the excursion to…	...אני רוצֶה לקחת את הסיור ב
	...אני רוצָה לקחת את הסיור ב
	ani rotze lakakhat et hasiyur be… **m**
	ani rotza lakakhat et hasiyur be… **f**
When's the next tour?	מתי הטיול הבא? *matay hatiyul haba?*
Are there tours in English?	יש טיולים באנגלית?
	yesh tiyulim be-anglit?
Is there an English guide book/ audio guide?	יש ספר הדרכה/מדריך קולי באנגלית?
	yesh sefer harakha/madrikh koli be-anglit?
What time do we leave/return?	באיזו שעה נעזוב/נחזור?
	be-eyzo sha-a na-azov/nakhazor?
We'd like to see…	...אנחנו רוצים לראות *anakhnu rotzim lir-ot*
Can we stop here…?	אפשר לעצור כאן..? *efshar la-atzor kan..?*
to take photos	כדי לצלם *kedey latzalem*
for souvenirs	לקנות מזכרות *liknot mazkarot*
for the toilets	להפסקת שרותים *lehafsakat sherutim*
Is it disabled-accessible?	האם יש גישה לנכים?
	ha-im yesh gisha lenekhim?

For Tickets, see page 19.

Seeing the Sights

Where's...?	?איפה...	*eyfo...?*
the botanical garden	הגן הבוטני	*hagan habotani*
the downtown	העיר התחתית	*ha-it hatakhtit*
the fountain	המעיין	*hama-ayan*
the Holy City	עיר הקודש	*ir hakodesh*
the Jewish Quarter	?הרובע היהודי	*harova hayehudi?*
the library	הספרייה	*hasifriya*
the market	השוק	*hashuk*
the museum	המוזיאון	*hamuze-on*
the old town	העיר העתיקה	*ha-ir ha-atika*
the opera house	בית האופרה	*beyt ha-opera*
the park	הפארק	*hapark*
the ruins	השרידים הארכאולוגיים	*hasridim ha-arkheologiyim*

the shopping area	אזור הקניות	*ezor hakniyot*
the town square	כיכר העיר	*kikar ha-ir*
the winery	היקב	*hayekev*
Can you show me on the map?	?אפשר להראות לי במפה	*efshar lehar-ot li bamapa?*
It's …	...זה	*ze…*
amazing	מדהים	*madhim*
beautiful	יפה	*yafe*
boring	משעמם	*mesha-amem*
interesting	מעניין	*me-anyen*
magnificent	מפואר	*mefo-ar*
romantic	רומנטי	*romanti*
strange	מוזר	*muzar*
terrible	נורא	*nora*
ugly	מכוער	*mekho-ar*
I (don't) like it	אהבתי (לא)	*(lo) ahavti*

For Asking Directions, see page 33.

Religious Sites

Where's…?	**?...איפה** *eyfo…?*
the shrine	מקום הפולחן
	mekom hapulkhan
the synagogue	בית הכנסת
	beyt hakneset
the temple	המקדש
	hamikdash
What time is the service?	?באיזה שעה התפילה *be-eyze sha-a hatfila?*

It is important to dress appropriately and modestly when
visiting religious sites or indeed the ultra-Orthodox quarters of
Me'a She'arim in Jerusalem and Bnei Brak near Tel Aviv. This is not a
quaint custom; those in violation of the edict may be sworn and spat
at, and even stoned.

Shopping

ESSENTIAL

Where's the market/ mall?	?השוק/הקניון *eyfo hashuk/hakenyon?*
I'm just looking.	.אני רק מסתכל. / אני רק מסתכלת *ani rak mistakel. **m** / ani rak mistakelet. **f***
Can you help me?	?אפשר לעזור לי *efshar la-azor li?*
I'm being helped.	.כבר עוזרים לי *kvar ozrim li.*
How much?	?כמה זה עולה *kama ze ole?*
That one, please.	.את זה, בבקשה *et ze, bevakasha.*
That's all.	.זה הכל *ze hakol.*
Where can I pay?	?איפה אפשר לשלם *eyfo efshar leshalem?*
I'll pay in cash/ by credit card.	.אני אשלם במזומן/ בכרטיס אשראי *ani ashalem bimezuman/bekartis ashray.*
A receipt, please.	.קבלה, בבקשה *kabala, bevakasha.*

Stores are usually open from 9:00 a.m. until 9:00 p.m., Sunday to Thursday, but close at 2:00 p.m. on Fridays and are closed all day Saturday.

At the Shops

Where's...?	?איפה...	eyfo...?
the antiques store	החנות לדברי עתיקות	hakhanut ledivrey atikot
the bakery	המאפייה	hama-afiya
the bank	הבנק	habank
the bookstore	חנות הספרים	khanut hasfarim
the clothing store	חנות הבגדים	khanut habgadim
the delicatessen	המעדנייה	hama-adaniya
the department	המחלקה	hamakhlaka
the gift shop	חנות המתנות	khanut hamatanot
the health food store	חנות הטבע	khanut hateva
the jeweller	חנות התכשיטים	khanut hatakhshitim
the liquor store [off-licence]	החנות למשקאות חריפים	hakhanut lemashka-ot kharifim
the market	השוק	hashuk
the music store	חנות המוזיקה	khanut hamuzika
the pastry shop	המאפייה	hama-afiya
the pharmacy	בית המרקחת	beyt hamirkakhat
the produce [grocery] store	המכולת	ha-makolet

the shoe store	חנות הנעליים	*khanut hana-alayim*
the shopping mall	הקניון	*ha-kanyon*
the souvenir store	חנות המזכרות	*khanut hamazkarot*
the supermarket	הסופרמרקט	*supermarket*
the tobacconist	חנות למוצרי טבק	*khanut lemutzrey tzbak*
the toy store	חנות הצעצועים	*khanut hatza-atzu-im*

Ask an Assistant

When do you open/close?	מתי אתם פותחים/סוגרים?	*matay atem potkhim/sogrim?*
the cashier	את הקופה	*et hakupa*
the escalator	את המדרגות הנעות	*et hamadregot hana-ot*
the elevator [lift]	את המעלית	*et hama-alit*
the fitting room	את חדר ההלבשה	*et kheder hahalbasha*
the store directory	את מדריך החנות	*et madrikh hakhanut*
Can you help me?	אפשר לעזור לי?	*efshar la-azor li?*
I'm just looking.	אני רק מסתכל. / אני רק מסתכלת.	*ani rak mistakel.* **m** / *ani rak mistakelet.* **f**
I'm being helped.	כבר עוזרים לי.	*kvar ozrim li.*
Do you have…?	יש לכם…?	*yesh lakem…?*

Can you show me…?	...?אפשר להראות לי
	efshar lehar-ot li…?
Can you ship/wrap it?	אפשר לשלוח/לעטוף את זה?
	cfshar lishlo-akh/la-atof et ze?
How much?	כמה זה עולה?
	kama ze ole?
That's all.	זה הכל. *ze hakol*

For Souvenirs, see page 131.

YOU MAY HEAR…

אפשר לעזור? *efshar la-azor?*	Can I help you?
רק רגע *rak rega*	One moment.
מה תרצה? / מה תרצי?	What would you like?
ma tirtze? **m** / *ma tirtzi?* **f**	
עוד משהו? *od mashehu?*	Anything else?

YOU MAY SEE...

פתוח/סגור	open/closed
בהפסקת צהריים	closed for lunch
חדר הלבשה	fitting room
קופה	cashier
מזומן בלבד	cash only
מכבדים כרטיסי אשראי	credit cards accepted
שעות הפתיחה	business hours
יציאה	exit

Personal Preferences

I'd like something...	אני רוצה משהו... / אני רוצה משהו...	
	*ani rotze mashehu... **m** / ani rotza mashehu... **f***	
cheap/expensive	זול/יקר	*zol/yakar*
larger/smaller	גדול/קטן יותר	*gadol/katan yoter*
from this region	מהאזור הזה	*meha-ezor haze*
Around...shekel.	בסביבות... שקל.	*besvivot... shekel.*
Is it real?	זה אמיתי?	*ze amiti?*
Can you show me	אפשר להראות לי את זה?	*efshar kehar-ot li at ze?*

That's not quite what I want.	זה לא בדיוק מה שרציתי.
	ze lo bediyuk ma sheratziti.
No, I don't like it.	לא, זה לא מוצא חן בעיניי.
	lo, ze lo motze khen be-eynay.
It's too expensive.	זה יקר מדי. *ze yakar miday.*
I have to think about it.	אני צריך לחשוב על זה. / אני צריכה לחשוב על זה.
	ani tzarikh lakhashov al ze. **m** /
	anı tzrıkha lkhashov al ze. **t**
I'll take it.	אני אקח את זה.
	ani ekakh et ze.

Paying & Bargaining

How much?	כמה זה עולה?
	kama ze ole?
I'll pay…	אני אשלם...
	ani ashalem…
in cash	במזומן
	bimezuman
by credit card	בכרטיס אשראי
	bekartis ashray
by traveler's cheque	בהמחאת נוסעים
	behamkha-at nos-im

YOU MAY HEAR...

איך תשלם? / איך תשלמי?
eykh teshalem? **m**/ *eykh teshalmi?* **f**

How are you paying?

כרטיס האשראי שלך נדחה.
/ כרטיס האשראי שלך נדחה.
kartis ha-ashray shelkha nidkha. **m** /
kartis ha-ashray shelakh nidkha. **f**

Your credit card has been declined.

תעודת זהות, בבקשה.
te-udat zehut, bevakasha.

ID please.

אנחנו לא מקבלים כרטיסי אשראי.
anakhnu lo mekablim kartisey ashray.

We don't accept credit cards.

מזומן בלבד בבקשה.
mezuman bilvad bevakasha.

Cash only, please.

A receipt, please.	קבלה, בבקשה. *kabala, bevakasha.*	
That's too much.	זה יותר מדי. *ze yoter miday.*	
I'll give you...	אני אתן לך... / אני אתן לך...	

	*ani eten lekha... **m** / ani eten lakh... **f***
I have only...shekel.	.יש לי רק... שקל
	yesh li rak... shekel.
Is that your best price?	?זה המחיר הכי טוב שלך / זה המחיר הכי טוב שלך
	ze hamekhir hakhi tov shelkha? **m** / *ze hamekhir hakhi*
	tov shelakh? **f**
Can you give me	?אפשר לקבל הנחה
a discount?	*efshar lekabel hanakha?*

For Numbers, see page 174.

Making a Complaint

I'd like...	אני רוצֶה... / אני רוצָה...	*ani rotze... **m** / ani rotza... **f***
to exchange this	להחליף את זה	*lehakhlif et ze*
a refund	החזר כספי	*hekhzer kaspi*
to see the manager	דבר עם המנהל	*ledaber im hamena-el*

In markets and sometimes in smaller stores, bargaining is the
name of the game. Avoid haggling though if you are not really
interested in buying or if an item is cheap.

Services

Can you recommend...?	?...אפשר לקבל המלצה לגבי *efshar lekabel hamlatza legabey...?*
a barber	ספר *sapar*
a dry cleaner	מכבסה לניקוי יבש *makhbesa lenikuy yavesh*
a hairstylist	מעצב שיער / מעצבת שיער *me-atzev se-ar **m** / me-atzevet se-ar **f***
a Laundromat [launderette]	מכבסה אוטומטית *makhbesa otomatit*
a nail salon	סלון יופי *salon yofi*
a spa	ספא *spa*
a travel agency	סוכנות נסיעות *sokhnut nesi-ot*
Can you ... this?	?אפשר... את זה *efshar... et ze?*
alter	לשנות *leshanot*
clean	לנקות *lenakot*
fix	לתקן *letaken*
press	ללחוץ *lilkhotz*
When will it be ready?	?מתי זה יהיה מוכן *matay ze ihiye mukhan?*

Hair & Beauty

I'd like...	‫אני רוצה... / אני רוצָה...‬	*ani rotze...* **m** / *ani rotza...* **f**
an appointment for	‫לקבוע תור להיום/למחר‬	
today/tomorrow		*likbo a tor lehayom/lemakhar*
some color/ highlights	‫קצת צבע/ גוונים‬	*ktzat tzeva/gvanim*
my hair styled/ blow-dried.	‫לעצב/לעשות פן לשיער שלי‬	*le-atzev/la-asot fen lase-ar sheli*
a haircut	‫תספורת‬	*tisporet*
an eyebrow/ bikini wax	‫לעשות שעווה בגבות/באזור הביקיני‬	*la-asot sha-ava bagabot/be-ezor habikini*
a facial	‫טיפול פנים‬	*tipul panim*
a manicure/ pedicure	‫מניקור/פדיקור‬	*manikur/pedikur*
a (sports) massage	‫עיסוי (ספורטאים)‬	*isuy (sporta-im)*
threading	‫הסרת שיער בחוט‬	*hasarat se-ar bekhut*
a trim, please.	‫גזימת הקצוות, בבקשה.‬	*gzimat haktzavot, bevakasha.*
Not too short.	‫לא יותר מדי קצר.‬	*lo yoter miday katzar.*
Shorter here.	‫קצר יותר כאן.‬	*katzar yoter kan.*
Do you offer....?	‫האם אתם מציעים...?‬	*ha-im atem matzi-im....?*
acupuncture	‫טיפול בדיקור‬	*tipul bedikur?*

aromatherapy	ארומתרפיה *aromaterapya*
oxygen	טיפול בחמצן *tipul bekhamtzan*
Is there a sauna/ steam room?	?האם יש חדר סאונה/ אדים *ha-im yesh kheder sa-una/edim?*

> The properties of the Dead Sea are extremely therapeutic.
> Among the minerals found in the water are bromine, which
> soothes the nerves, and iodine and magnesium, which ease arthritis,
> rheumatism, psoriasis and skin problems, as well as respiratory
> complaints. There are also sulphur baths in Ein Gedi and Ein Bokek.

Antiques

How old is it?	?עד כמה זה ישן *ad kama ze yashan?*
Do you have anything from the...period?	?...יש לכם משהו מתקופת ה *yesh lakhem mashehu mitkufat ha...?*
Do I have to fill out any forms?	?האם עלי למלא איזשהו טופס *ha-im alay lemale eyzeshehu tofes?*
Is there a certificate of authenticity?	?יש תעודת מקוריות *yesh te-udat mekoriyut?*
Can you ship/ wrap it?	אפשר לשלוח / לעטוף את זה? *efshar lishlo-akh/la-atof et ze?*

Clothing

I'd like…	אני רוצֶה… / אני רוצָה… *ani rotze…* **m** / *ani rotza…* **f**
Can I try this on?	אפשר לנסות את זה? *efshar lenasot et ze?*
It doesn't fit.	זה לא מתאים. *ze lo mat-im.*
It's too…	זה … מדי. *ze… miday.*
big/small	גדול/קטן *gadol/katan*
short/long	קצר/ארוך *katzar/arokh*
tight/loose	צמוד/רפוי *tzamus/rafuy*
Do you have this in size…?	יש לכם את זה במידה…? *yesh lakhem et ze bemida…?*
Do you have this in a bigger/smaller size?	יש לכם את זה במידה גדולה/קטנה יותר? *yesh lakhem et benida gdola/ktana yoter?*

For Numbers, see page 174.

YOU MAY HEAR…

זה נראה יופי עליך. / זה נראה יופי עלייך.
ze nir-a yofi aleykha. **m** / *ze nir-a yofi alayikh.* **f**
That looks great on you.

איך זה עולה? *eykh ze ole?*
How does it fit?

אין לנו את זה במידה שלךָ.
אין לנו את זה במידה שלךְ.
eyn lanu et ze bamida shelkha. **m** /
eyn lanu et ze bamida shelakh. **f**
We don't have your size.

Dress code can be very confusing in Israel. In Tel Aviv, it's a case of "if you've got it, flaunt it", while in Jerusalem and Arabic locations, modest dress is advisable.
Sephardic Jews can be fussy about footwear, favoring closed-toe shoes. It is considered rude to put your feet up on tables and chairs.

YOU MAY SEE...

גברים	men's clothing
נשים	women's clothing
ילדים	children's clothing

Colors

I'd like something...	אני רוצה משהו... / אני רוצה משהו...
	*ani rotze mashehu... **m** / ani rotza mashehu... **f***
beige	בבז *bebezh*
black	בשחור *beshakhor*
blue	בכחול *bekakhol*
brown	בחום *bekhum*
green	בירוק *beyarok*
gray	באפור *be-afor*
orange	בכתום *bekatom*
pink	בוורוד *bevarod*
purple	בסגול *besagol*
red	באדום *be-adom*
white	בלבן *belavan*
yellow	בצהוב *betzahov*

Clothes & Accessories

a backpack	תרמיל גב	*tarmil gav*
a belt	חגורה	*khagora*
a bikini	ביקיני	*bikini*
a blouse	חולצה	*khultza*
a bra	חזייה	*khaziya*
briefs [underpants]/	תחתוני גברים/תחתוני נשים	
panties (ladies)	*takhtoney gvarim/takhtoney nashim*	
a coat	מעיל	*me-il*
a dress	שמלה	*simla*
a hat	כובע	*kova*
a jacket	ז׳קט	*zhaket*
jeans	ג׳ינס	*jins*
pyjamas	פיג׳מה	*pijama*
pants [trousers]	מכנסיים	*mikhnasayim*
pantyhose [tights]	גרבי ניילון	*garbey naylon*
a purse [handbag]	תיק יד	*tik yad*
a raincoat	מעיל גשם	*me-il geshem*
a scarf	צעיף	*tza-if*
a shirt	חולצה	*khultza*
shorts	מכנסיים קצרים	*mikhnasayim ktzarim*
a skirt	חצאית	*khatza-it*

socks	גרביים *garbayim*
a suit	חליפה *khalifa*
sunglasses	משקפי שמש *mishkafey shemesh*
a sweater	סוודר *sveder*
a sweatshirt	חולצת סווטשירט *khultzat svetshert*
a swimsuit	בגד ים *beged yam*
a T-shirt	חולצת טריקו *khultzat triko*
a tie	עניבה *aniva*
underwear	תחתונים *takhtonim*

Fabric

I'd like...	...אני רוצֶה... / אני רוצָה *ani rotze...* **m** / *ani rotza...* **f**
cotton	מכותנה *mikutna*
denim	מג'ינס *mejins*
lace	מתחרה *mitakhara*
leather	מעור *me-or*
linen	מפשתן *mepishtan*
silk	ממשי *mimeshi*
wool	מצמר *mitzemer*
Is it machine washable?	?אפשר לכבס את זה במכונה *efshar lekhabes et ze bemekhona?*

Shoes

I'd like…	אני רוצֶה... / אני רוצָה...	
	*ani rotze… **m** / ani rotza… **f***	
high-heels/flats	עקב גבוה/שטוח	*akev gavoha/shatu-akh*
boots	מגפיים	*magafayim*
loafers	נעלי לופרס	*na-aley lofers*
sandals	סנדלים	*sandalim*
shoes	נעליים	*na-alayim*
slippers	נעלי בית	*na-aley bayit*
sneakers	נעלי התעמלות	*na-aley hit-amlut*
size…	גודל...	*godel…*

For Numbers, see page 174.

Sizes

Small (S)	(S)קטן	*katan (S)*
Medium (M)	(M)מדיום	*medyum (M)*
Large (L)	(L)לארג'	*larj (L)*
Extra Large	(XL)אקסטרה לארג'	*ekstra larj (XL)*
Petite	פטיט	*petit*
Plus size	מידות גדולות	*midot gdolot*

Newsagent & Tobacconist

Do you sell English-language newspapers?	?האם אתם מוכרים עיתונים באנגלית *ha-im atem mokhrim itonim be-anglit?*
I'd like...	...אני רוצֶה / ...אני רוצָה *ani rotze... **m** /ani rotza... **f***
candy [sweets]	ממתקים *mamtakim*
chewing gum	מסטיק *mastik*
a chocolate bar	שוקולד *shokolad*
a cigar	סיגר *sigar*
a pack/carton of cigarettes	חפיסת/קרטון סיגריות *khafisat/karton sigaryot*
a lighter	מצית *matzit*
a magazine	כתב עת *ktav et*
matches	גפרורים *gafrurim*
a newspaper	עיתון *iton*
a pen	עט *et*
a postcard	גלויה *gluya*
a road/town map of...	...מפת כבישים/העיר של *mapat kvishim/ha-ir shel...*
stamps	בולים *bulim*

Photography

I'd like…camera.	אני רוצֶה מצלמה… / אני רוצָה מצלמה…	
	*ani rotze matzlema… **m** / ani rotza matzlema… **f***	
an automatic	אוטומטית	*otomatit*
a digital	דיגיטלית	*digitalit*
a disposable	חד פעמית	*khad pe-amit*
I'd like…	אני רוצֶה…/ אני רוצָה…	
	*ani rotze… **m** / ani rotza… **f***	
a battery	סוללה	*solela*
digital prints	תדפיסים דיגיטליים	*tadpisim digitaliyim*
a memory card	כרטיס זיכרון	*kartis zikaron*
Can I print digital photos here?	אפשר לקבל כאן תמונות דיגיטליות?	
	efshar lekabel kan tmunot digitaliyot?	

Souvenirs

A bottle of wine.	בקבוק יין	*bakbuk yayin*
A box of chocolates.	דלוקוש תריינובנוב	*bonbonyerat shokolad*
Some crystal.	בדולחים	*bedolakhim*
A doll.	בובה	*buba*
Some jewellery.	תכשיטים	*takhshitim*
a key ring.	מחזיק מפתחות	*makhzik maftekhot*

a postcard.	גלויה *gluya*
some pottery.	כלי חרס *kley kheres*
a T-shirt.	חולצת טריקו *khultzat triko*
a toy.	צעצוע *tza-atzu-a*
Can I see this/that?	?אפשר לראות את זה *efshar lir-ot et ze?*
I'd like…	...אני רוצֶה / אני רוצָה *ani rotze… m / ani rotza… f*
a battery	סוללה *solela*
a bracelet	צמיד *tzamid*
a brooch	סיכה לבגד *sika lebeged*
a clock	שעון קיר *she-on kir*
earrings	עגילים *agilim*
a necklace	מחרוזת *makhrozet*
a ring	טבעת *taba-at*
a watch	שעון יד *she-on yad*
I'd like…	...אני רוצֶה / אני רוצָה *ani rotze… m / ani rotza… f*
copper	נחושת *nekhoshet*
crystal	בדולח *bedolakh*

diamonds	יהלומים	*yahalomim*
white/yellow gold	זהב לבן/צהוב	*zahav lavan/tzahov*
pearls	פנינים	*pninim*
pewter	פיוטר	*pyuter*
platinum	פלטינה	*platina*
sterling silver	כסף סטרלינג	*keset sterling*
Is this real?	זה אמיתי?	*ze amiti?*
Can you engrave this?	אפשר לחרוט על זה?	*efhshar lakharot al ze?*

Antiquities offered by street urchins in Jerusalem are usually genuine. Although not of museum quality, they make a nice souvenir. Other typical arts and crafts include Bedouin embroidered bags, pillows and tablecloths, and Armenian pottery.

Sport & Leisure

ESSENTIAL

When's the game?	מתי המשחק?	matay hamiskhak
Where's...?	איפה...?	eyfo...?
the beach	חוף הים	khof hayam
the park	הפארק	hapark
the pool	הבריכה	habreykha
Is it safe to swim here?	זה בטוח לשחות כאן?	ze batu-akh liskhot kan?
Can I hire clubs?	אפשר לשכור מחבטים?	efshar liskor makhbetim?
How much per hour/day?	כמה זה עולה לשעה/ליום?	kama ze ole lesha-a/leyom?
How far is it to...?	עד כמה זה רחוק מ...?	ad kama ze rakhok me...?
Show me on the map, please.	תראה לי במפה, בבקשה. / תראי לי במפה בבקשה.	tar-e li bamapa, bevakasha. **m** / tar-i li baamapa, bevakasha. **f**

Watching Sport

When's...(game/race/tournament)?	מתי (משחק/מירוץ/טורניר)...?	matay (miskhak, meyrotz, turnir)...?
the baseball	הבייסבול	habeysbol
the basketball	הכדורסל	hakadursal
the boxing	האיגרוף	ha-igruf
the cricket	הקריקט	hakriket
the cycling	מירוץ האופניים	meyrotz ha-ofanayim
the golf	הגולף	hagolf

the soccer [football]	הכדורגל *hakaduregel*
the tennis	הטניס *hatenis*
the volleyball	הכדור־עף *hakadur af*
Who's playing?	?מי משחק *mi mesakhek?*
Where's the racetrack/stadium?	?איפה מסלול המירוצים/האיצטדיון eyfo maslul hameyrotzim/ha-itztadyon?*
Where can I place a bet?	?איפה אפשר להמר *eyfo efshar lehamer?*

For Tickets, see page 19.

Soccer is the number one spectator sport, with several matches every week. Basketball is also very popular.

Playing Sport

Where is/are...?	?...איפה יש *eyfo yesh...?*
the golf course	מגרש גולף *migrash golf*
the gym	חדר כושר *kheder kosher*
the park	פארק *park*

the tennis courts	מגרשי טניס	migrashey tenis
How much per...	כמה זה עולה ל....	kama ze ole le....
day	יום	yom
hour	שעה	sha-a
game	משחק	miskhak
round	סיבוב	sivuv
Can I rent [hire]...?	האם אפשר לשכור...?	ha-im efshar liskor...?
some clubs	מחבטים	makhbetim
some equipment	ציוד	tziyud
a racket	מחבט	makhbet

At the Beach/Pool

Where's the beach/pool?	איפה חוף הים/הבריכה?	eyfo khof hayam/habrekha
Is there a...?	האם יש...?	ha-im yesh...?
Kiddie pool	בריכה לילדים	brekha liyeladim
Indoor/outdoor pool	בריכה מקורה/חיצונית	brekha mekura/khitzonnit
Lifeguard	מציל	matzil
Is it safe...?	האם זה בטוח...?	ha-im ze batu-akh...?
to swim	לשחות	liskhot
to dive	לצלול	litzlol
for children	לילדים	lyeladim

I'd like to hire...	...אני רוצה לשכור / ...אני רוצֶה לשכּור	
	ani rotze liskor... **m** / ani rotza liskor... **f**	
a deck chair	כיסא נוח	kise no-akh
diving equipment	ציוד צלילה	tziud tzlila
a jet ski	אופנוע ים	ofano-a yam
a motorboat	סירת מנוע	sirat mano-a
a rowboat	סירת משוטים	sirat meshotim
snorkelling equipment	ציוד שנורקלינג	tziyud snorkeling
a surfboard	גלשן גלים	galshan galim
a towel	מגבת	magevet
an umbrella	מטרייה	mitriya
water skis	מגלשי מים	magleshey mayim
a windsurfing board	גלשן רוח	galshan ru-akh
For...hours.	ל... שעות	le... sha-ot

Tel Aviv has 14km (9 miles) of beaches. The beach near Tel Aviv port is segregated for religious bathers.

YOU MAY SEE...

מעליות	lifts
מעליות משיכה	drag lift
רכבל	cable car
רכבל מושב	chair lift
למתחילים	novice
למתקדמים	intermediate
למומחים	expert
המסלול סגור	trail [piste] closed

Winter Sports

A lift pass for a day/ five days, please.	סקי פס ליום/לחמישה ימים, בבקשה. *ski pas leyom/lekhamisha yamim, bevakasha.*
I'd like to hire...	אני רוצֶה לשכור... / אני רוצָה לשכור... *ani rotze liskor...* **m** / *ani rotza liskor...* **f**
boots	מגפיים *magafayim*
a helmet	קסדה *kasda*
poles	מוטות סקי *motot ski*
skis	מגלשי סקי *magleshey ski*
a snowboard	גלשן שלג *galshan sheleg*
snowshoes	נעלי שלג *na-aley sheleg*
These are too big/ small.	אלה גדולים/קטנים יותר מדי. *ele gdolim/ktanim yoter miday.*
Are there lessons?	האם יש שיעורים? *ha-im yesh she-urim?*
I'm a beginner.	אני מתחיל. / אני מתחילה. *ani matkhil.* **m** / *ani matkhila.* **f**
I'm experienced.	אני מנוסֶה. / אני מנוסָה. *ani menuse.* **m** / *ani menusa.* **f**
A trail map, please.	מפת מסלולים, בבקשה. *mapat maslulim, bevakasha.*

Out in the Country

A map of..., please.	מפה של..., בבקשה.	
	mapa shel..., bevakasha.	
this region	האזור הזה	*ha-ezor haze*
the walking routes	שבילי ההליכה	
	shviley hahalikha	
the bike routes	שבילי אופניים	
	shviley ofanayim	
the trails	המסלולים	*hamaslulim*
Is it...?	האם זה...?	*ha-im ze...?*
easy	קל	*kal*
difficult	קשה	*kashe*
far	רחוק	*rakhok*
steep	תלול	*talul*
How far is it to?	עד כמה זה רחוק מ...?	
	ad kama ze rakhok me...?	
I'm lost.	הלכתי לאיבוד.	
	halakhti le-ibud	
Where's...?	איפה...?	*eyfo...?*
the bridge	הגשר	*hagesher*
the cave	המערה	*hame-ara*

the desert	המידבר
	hamidbar
the farm	החווה
	hakhava
the field	השדה
	hasade
the forest	היער *haya-ar*
the hill	הגבעה *hagiv-a*
the mountain	ההר *hahar*
the nature preserve	שמורת הטבע
	shmurat hateva
the viewpoint	נקודת התצפית
	nekudat hatatzpit
the park	הפארק
	hapark
the path	השביל
	hashvil
the peak	הגספה
	hapisga
the picnic area	אזור הפיקניק
	ezor hapiknik
the river	הנהר *hanahar*
the sea	הים *hayam*
the (hot) spring	המעיינות (החמים)
	hama-ayanot (hakhamim)
the stream	הנחל
	hanakhal
the valley	העמק
	ha-emek
the vineyard	היקב
	hayekev

Going Out

ESSENTIAL

What's there to do at night?	מה יש לעשות בלילה?	*ma yesh la-asot balayla?*
Do you have a program of events?	יש לכם תוכנית אירועים?	*yesh lakhem tokhnit eyru-im*
What's playing tonight?	מה מציג הלילה?	*ma matzig halayla?*
Where's...?	...איפה?	*eyfo...?*
the downtown area	אזור העיר התחתית	*ezor ha-ir hatakhtit*
the bar	הבר	*habar*
the dance club	מועדון הריקודים	*mo-adon harikudim*

Entertainment

Can you recommend...?	?...אפשר לקבל המלצה לגבי	*efshar lekabel hamlatza legabey...?*
a concert	העפוה	*hofa-a*
a movie	סרט	*seret*
an opera	אופרה	*opera*
a play	מחזה	*makhaze*
When does it start/end?	מתי זה מתחיל/נגמר?	*matay ze matkhil/nigmar?*
What's the dress code?	מה קוד הלבוש?	*ma kod halevush?*
I like...	אני אוהב... / אני אוהבת...	*ani ohev... **m** / ani ohevet... **f***
classical music	מוזיקה קלסית	*muzika klasit*
folk music	מוזיקת פולקלור	*musikat folklor*
jazz	ג'אז	*jez*
pop music	מוזיקת פופ	*muzikat pop*
rap	ראפ	*rap*

Nightlife

What's there to do at night?	מה יש לעשות בלילה?
	ma yesh la-asot balayla?
Can you recommend...?	אפשר לקבל המלצה לגבי...?
	efshar lekabel hamlatza legabey...?
a bar	בר *bar*
a cabaret	הופעת קברט
	hofa-at kabaret
a casino	קזינו *kazino*
a dance club	מועדון ריקודים
	mo-adon rikudim
a gay club	מועדון לעליזים
	mo-adon le-alizim
a jazz club	מועדון ג'אז *mo-adon jez*

Nighlife starts late in Israel — usually from 11:00 p.m. onwards. Thursday night is the big night out.

YOU MAY HEAR...

נא לכבות את הטלפונים הסלולריים שלכם.
na lekhabot et hatelefonim haselolariyim shelakhem.

Turn off your cell [mobile] phones, please.

a club with local music	מועדון עם מוזיקה מקומית *mo-adon im muzika mekomit*
Is there live music?	יש מוזיקה חיה? *yesh muzika khaya?*
How do I get there?	איך מגיעים לשם? *eykh magi-im lesham?*
Is there a cover charge?	האם יש דמי כניסה? *ha-im yesh dmey knisa?*
Let's go dancing.	בוא נלך לרקוד. / בואי נלך לרקוד. *bo nelekh lirkod. m / bo-i nelekh lirkod. m*
Is this area safe at night?	האם האזור הזה בטוח בלילה? *ha-im ha-ezor haze batu-akh balayla?*

Special
Requirements

Business Travel

ESSENTIAL

I'm here on business.	אני כאן בענייני עסקים. *ani kan be-inyaney asakim.*
Here's my card.	הנה הכרטיס שלי. *hine hakartis sheli.*
Can I have your card?	וְלש סיטרכה תא לבקל רשפא? וְלש סיטרכה תא לבקל רשפא? *efshar lekabel et hakartis shelkha?* **m** *efshar lekabel et hakartis shelakh?* **f**
I have a meeting with...	יש לי פגישה עם... *yesh li pgisha im...*
Where's...?	איפה...? *eyfo...?*
the business center	מרכז העסקים *merkaz ha-asakim*
the convention hall	אולם הוועידות *ulam have-idot*
the meeting room	חדר הפגישות *kheder hapgishot*

Tourists should stick to general greetings such as **shalom** (hello) and **lehitra-ot** (goodbye). It is usual to shake hands when you first meet someone, though you should wait for them to offer their hand first in case they are prevented from doing so because of a religious custom.

On Business

I'm here for...	אני כאן ל... *ani kan le...*
a seminar	יום עיון *yom iyun*
a conference	ועידה *ve-ida*
a meeting	פגישה *pgisha*

My name is...	השם שלי הוא... *hashem sheli hu...*
May I introduce my colleague...	אני רוצֶה להציג את העמית שלי... אני רוצֶה להציג את העמיתה שלי... *ani rotze m lehatzig et ha-amit m sheli... /* *ani rotza f lehatzig et ha-amita f sheli...*
I have a meeting/an appointment with...	יש לי ישיבה/ פגישה עם... *yesh li yeshiva/pgisha im...*
I'm sorry I'm late.	סליחה על האיחור. *slikha al ha-ikhur.*
I need an interpreter.	אני צריך מתורגמן. / אני צריכה מתורגמן. *ani tzarikh meturgeman m / ani tzrikha meturgeman f*
You can contact me at the...Hotel.	אפשר ליצור אתי קשר במלון... *efshar litzor iti kesher bamalon...*
I'm here until...	אני כאן עד... *ani kan ad...*
I need to...	אני צריך... / אני צריכה... *ani tzarikh... m / ani tzrikha... f*
make a call	לעשות שיחת טלפון *la-asot sikhat telefon*
make a photocopy	לעשות צילום *la-asot tzilum*
send an email	לשלוח אימייל *lishlo-akh email*
send a fax	לשלוח פקס *lishlo-akh fax*
send a package (for next-day delivery)	לשלוח חבילה (למשלוח מהיום-למחר) *lishlo-akh khavila (lemishlo-akh mehayom lemakhar)*
It was a pleasure to meet you.	אני שמחתי להכיר אותך. / אני שמחתי להכיר אותך. *ani samakhti lehakir otkha. m / ani samakhti lehakir otakh. f*

For Communications, see page 48.

YOU MAY HEAR...

יש לך פגישה? / יש לך פגישה?
yesh lekha pgisha? **m** */ yesh lakh pgisha?* **f**

עם מי? *im mi?*

הוא/היא בישיבה.
hu/hi beyeshiva.

רק רגע, בבקשה. *rak rega, bevakasha.*

שב, בבקשה. / שבי, בבקשה.
shev, bevakasha. **m** */ shvi, bevakasha.* **f**

אתה רוצה לשתות משהו? /
את רוצה לשתות משהו?
ata rotze lishtot masheho? **m** */ at rotza lishtot masheho?* **f**

תודה שבאתָ. / תודה שבאת.
toda shebata. **m** */ toda shebat.* **f**

Do you have an
appointment?
With whom?
He/She is in a meeting.

One moment, please.
Have a seat.

Would you like something
to drink?

Thank you for coming.

Traveling with Children

ESSENTIAL

Is there a discount for kids?	יש הנחה לילדים?
	yesh hanakha liyeladim?
Can you recommend a babysitter?	אפשר להמליץ על בייביסיטר?
	efshar lehamlitz al beybi siter
Do you have a child's seat/highchair?	יש לכם מושב/כיסא האכלה לילדים?
	yesh lakhem moshav/kise ha-akhala liyeladim?
Where can I change the baby?	איפה אוכל להחליף לתינוק?
	איפה אוכל להחליף לתינוקת?
	*eyfo ukhal lekhlif latinok? **m** / eyfo ukhal lehakhlif latinoket? **f***

Out & About

Can you recommend something for the kids?	אפשר להמליץ על משהו לילדים?
	efshar lehamlitz al mashehu liyeladim?
Where's...?	איפה...? *eyfo...?*
the amusement	פארק השעשועים *park hasha-ashu-im*
the arcade	הארקדה *ha-arkada*
the kiddie [paddling] pool	בריכת הילדים *brekhat hayeladim*
the park	הפארק *hapark*
the playground	מגרש המשחקים *migrash hamiskhakim*
the zoo	גן החיות *gan hakhayot*
Are kids allowed?	האם הכניסה מותרת לילדים?
	ha-im haknisa muteret liyeladim?
Is it safe for kids?	האם זה בטוח לילדים?
	ha-im ze batu-akh liyeladim?

Is it suitable for...	...?האם זה מתאים לילדים בגיל
year olds?	*ha-im ze mat-im liyeladim begil...?*

For Numbers, see page 174.

YOU MAY HEAR...

איזה מתוק! *eyze matok!*
?איך קוראים לו / לה
*eykh kor-im lo? **m** / la? **f***

How cute!
What's his/her name?

?איה המכ תב / ?אוה המכ ןב
*ben kama hu? **m** / bat kama hi? **f***

How old is he/she?

Baby Essentials

Do you have...?	...?יש לכם *yesh lakhem...?*
a baby bottle	בקבוק לתינוק *bakbuk latinok*
baby food	אוכל לתינוקות *okhel letinokot*
baby wipes	מגבונים לתינוק *magvonim latinok*
a car seat	מושב בטיחות *moshav betikhut*

a children's menu/portion	תפריט/מנה לילדים tafrit/mana liyeladim
a child's seat highchair	מושב/כיסא האכלה לילד moshav/kise ha-akhala layeld
a crib/cot	עריסה/מיטה מתקפלת arisa/mita mitkapelet
diapers [nappies]	חיתולים khitulim
formula	פורמולה formula
a pacifier [dummy]	מוצץ motzetz
a playpen	לול לתינוקות lul letinokot
a stroller [pushchair]	עגלת ילדים eglat yeladim
Can I breastfeed the baby here?	תא קינהל רשפא / ?ןאכ קוניתה תא קינהל רשפא? efshar kehanik et hatinok **m** kan? / ןאכ תקוניתה efshar lehanik et hatinoket **f** kan?
Where can I breastfeed/change the baby?	?קוניתל ףילחהל/קינהל רשפא הפיא ?תקוניתל ףילחהל/קינהל רשפא הפיא eyfo efshar lehanik/lehakhlif latinok **m** / eyfo efshar lehanik/lehakhlif latinoket **f** ?

For Dining with Children, see page 64.

Babysitting

Can you recommend a babysitter?	?רטיסיביב לע ץילמהל רשפא efshar lehamlitz al beybi sitter?
How much do you/ they charge?	?מה התערי/ךלש/ךלש/שלהד ma hata-arif shelkha **m** / shelakh **f** / shelakhem **pl**
I'll be back at...	...העשב רוזחא ekhzor be-sha-a...
If you need contact me, call...	...רפסמב ינא ,יתא רשק רוציל ךירצ םא im tzarikh litzor kesher iti, ani bamispar...

For Time, see page 176.

Health & Emergency

Can you recommend a pediatrician?	?אפשר להמליץ על רופא ילדים *efshar lehamlitz al rofe yeladim?*
My child is allergic to…	...הילד שלי אלרגי ל... / חילדה שלי אלרגית ל *hayeled sheli alergi le… **m** / hayalda sheli alergit le… **f***
My child is missing.	הילד שלי נעדר. / הילדה שלי נעדרת. *hayeled sheli ne-edar. **m** / hayalda sheli ne-ederet. **f***
Have you seen a boy/girl?	?האם ראיתָ / ראית ילד/ילדה *ha-im ra-ita **m** / ra-it **f** yeled/yalda?*

For Health, see page 159.

For Police, see page 156.

Disabled Travelers

ESSENTIAL

Is there...?	?...האם יש	ha-im yesh...?
access for the disabled	גישה לנכים	gisha lenekhim
a wheelchair ramp	רמפה לכיסא גלגלים	rampa lekise galgalim
a disabled-accessible toilet	בית שימוש לנכים	beyt shimush lenekhim
I need...	אני צריך... / אני צריכה...	ani tzarikh... **m** / ani tzrikha... **f**
assistance	עזרה	ezra
an elevator [a lift]	מעלית	ma-alit
a ground-floor room	חדר בקומת קרקע	kheder bekomat karka

Asking for Assistance

I'm...	אני...	ani...
disabled	נכה / נכה	nekhe **m** / nekha **f**
visually impaired	לקוי ראיה / לקוית ראיה	lekuy re-iya **m** / lekuyat re-iya **f**
deaf	חרש / חרשת	kheresh **m** / khereshet **f**
hearing impaired	לקוי שמיעה / לקוית שמיעה	lekuy shmi-a **m** / lekuyat shmi-a **f**
unable to walk far/ use the stairs	לא יכול / יכולה ללכת רחוק/להשתמש במדרגות	lo yakhol **m** / yekhola **f** lalekhet rakhok/lehishtamesh bamadregot

Please speak louder.	בבקשה לדבר בקול רם יותר. *bevakasha ledaber bekol ram yoter.*
Can I bring my wheelchair?	אפשר להביא את כיסא הגלגלים שלי? *efshar lehavi et kise hagalgalim sheli?*
Are guide dogs permitted?	אפשר להביא כלבי נחיה? *efshar lehavi kalbey nekhiya?*
Can you help me?	אפשר לעזור לי? *efshar la-azor li?*
Please open/ hold the door.	בבקשה לפתוח/להחזיק את הדלת. *bevakasha lifto-akh/lehakhzik et hadelet.*

For Health, see page 159.

In an Emergency

Emergencies

ESSENTIAL

Help!	הצילו!	
	hatzilu!	
Go away!	לך מפה! / לכי מפה!	
	lekh mipo! **m** / *lekhi mipo!* **f**	
Stop, thief!	עצור, גנב!	
	atzor, ganav!	
Get a doctor!	תקרא לרופא! / תקראי לרופא!	
	tikra lerofe! **m** / *tikre-i lerofe!* **f**	
Fire!	אש! *esh!*	
I'm lost.	הלכתי לאיבוד.	
	halakhti le-ibud.	
Can you help me?	אפשר לעזור לי?	
	efshar la-azor li?	

In an emergency, dial:

100 for the police

101 for an ambulance

102 for the fire brigade.

103 for the electricity company.

Police

ESSENTIAL

Call the police!	תתקשר למשטרה! / תתקשרי למשטרה!
	titkasher lamishtara! **m** / *titkashri lamishtara!* **f**
Where's the police station?	איפה תחנת המשטרה?
	eyfo takhanat hamishtara?
There was an accident/attack.	הייתה תאונה/התקפה.
	hayta te-una/hatkafa.
My child is missing.	הילד שלי נעדר. / הילדה שלי נעדרת.
	hayeled sheli ne-edar. **m** / *hayalda sheli ne-ederet.* **f**
I need...	אני צריך... / אני צריכה...
	ani tzarikh... **m** / *ani tzrikha...* **f**
an interpreter	מתורגמן
	meturgeman
to make a phone call.	לעשות שיחה טלפונית
	la-asot sikha telefonit
I'm innocent.	אני חף מפשע. / אני חפה מפשע.
	ani khaf mipesha. **m** / *ani khafa mipesha.* **f**

By dialling *3888 from any phone, tourists can seek information and assistance regarding tourist services as well as assistance from the police, Ministry of Interior Services, Airport Authority, and more.

YOU MAY HEAR...

מלא את הטופס הזה, בבקשה.
מלאי את הטופס הזה בבקשה.
male et hatofes haze bevakasha. m
mal-i et hatofes haze bevakasha. f

Fill out this form.

תעודת הזהות שלך בבקשה.
תעודת הזהות שלך, בבקשה.
te-udat hazehut shelkh, bevakasha. m
te-udat hazehut shelakh, bevakasha. f

ID, please.

מתי/איפה זה קרה?
matay/eyfo ze kara?

איך הוא/היא נראה/נראית?
eykh hu/hi nir-a/nir-et?

When/Where did it
happen?
What does he/she
look like?

Crime & Lost Property

I need to report...   ...אני צריך לדווח על... / אני צריכה לדווח על
ani tzarikh ledave-akh al... m /
ani tzrikha ledave-akh al... f

a mugging	שוד	shod
a rape	אונס	ones
a theft	גניבה	gneyva
I was mugged.	נשדדתי.	nishdadeti.
I was robbed.	נשדדתי.	nishdadeti.
I lost...	איבדתי את...	ibadeti et...
...was stolen.	נגנב... / נגנבה... / נגנבו...	nignav... m / nigneva... f / nignevu... pl

My backpack	תרמיל הגב שלי	tarmil hagav sheli m
My bicycle	האופניים שלי	ha-ofanayim sheli
My camera	המצלמה שלי	hamatzlema sheli f
My (hire) car	המכונית (השכורה) שלי	hamekhonit (haskhura) sheli f
My computer	המחשב שלי	hamakhshev sheli m
My credit card	כרטיס האשראי שלי	kartis ha-ashray sheli m
My jewelry	התכשיטים שלי	hatakhshitim sheli pl
My money	הכסף שלי	hakesef sheli m
My passport	הדרכון שלי	hadarkon sheli m
My purse [handbag]	תיק היד שלי	tik hayad sheli m
My traveler's cheques	המחאות הנוסעים שלי	hamkha-ot hanos-im sheli pl
My wallet	הארנק שלי	ha-arnak sheli m
I need a police report.	אני צריך דו"ח משטרתי. / אני צריכה דו"ח משטרתי.	ani tzarikh dokh mishtarti. m / ani tzrikha dokh mishtarti. f
Where is the British/ American/Irish embassy?	איפה השגרירות הבריטית/האמריקאית/האירית?	eyfo hashagrirut habritit/ha-amerika-it/ha-irit?

Health

ESSENTIAL

I'm sick.	אני חולֶה. / אני חולָה. *ani khole* **m** / *ani khola* **f**
I need an English-speaking doctor.	אני צריך רופא שמדבר אנגלית. אני צריכה רופא שמדבר אנגלית. *ani tzarikh rofe shemedaber anglit.* **m** / *ani tzrikha rofe shemedaber anglit.* **f**
It hurts here.	כואב כאן. *ko-ev kan.*

Finding a Doctor

Can you recommend a doctor/dentist?	אפשר להמליץ על רופא/רופא שיניים? *efshar lehamlitz al rofe/rofe shinayim?*
Can the doctor come here?	האם הרופא יכול לבוא לכאן? *ha-im harofe yakhol lavo lekan?*
I need an English-speaking doctor.	אני צריך רופא שמדבר אנגלית. אני צריכה רופא שמדבר אנגלית. *ani tzarikh rofe shemedaber anglit.* **m** / *ani tzrikha rofe shemedaber anglit.* **f**
What are the office hours?	מהן שעות הפתיחה? *mahen sh-ot haptikha?*
I'd like an appointment for...	אני רוצֶה תור ל... / אני רוצה תור ל... *ani rotze tor le...* **m** / *ani rotza tor le...* **f**
today	היום *hayom*
tomorrow	מחר *makhar*
as soon as possible	בהקדם האפשרי *bahekdem ha-efshari*
It's urgent.	זה דחוף. *ze dakhuf.*

Symptoms

I'm bleeding.	אני מדמם. / אני מדממת.	
	*ani medamem **m** / ani medamemet **f***	
I'm constipated.	יש לי עצירות.	
	yesh li atzirut.	
I'm dizzy.	יש לי סחרחורת.	
	yesh li skharkhoret.	
I'm nauseous.	יש לי בחילה.	
	yesh li bkhila.	
I'm vomiting	אני מקיא. / אני מקיאה.	
	*ani meki. **m** / ani meki-a. **f***	
It hurts here.	כואב כאן. *ko-ev kan*	
I have...	יש לי... *yesh li...*	
an allergic	תגובה אלרגית	
reaction	*tguva alergit*	
chest pain	כאבים בחזה *ke-evim bakhaze*	
cramps	התכווצויות *hitkavtzuyot*	
diarrhea	שלשול *hilshul*	
an earache	כאב באוזן *ke-ev ba-ozen*	
a fever	חום *khom*	
pain	כאבים *ke-evim*	

a rash	פריחה prikha
a sprain	נקע neka
some swelling	התנפחות hitnapkhut
a sore throat	כאב גרון ke-ev garon
a stomach ache	כאב בטן ke-ev beten
I've been sick	אני הייתי חולה /אני הייתי חולה
	ani hayiti khole /ani hayiti khola
for...days.	במשך... ימים. /במשך... ימים.
	bemeshekh... yamim. **m** /bemeshekh... yamim **f**

For Numbers, see page 174.

Conditions

I'm...	אני... ani...
anemic	אנמי / אנמית anemi **m** / anemit **f**
asthmatic	אסתמטי / אסתמטית astmati **m** / astmatit **f**
diabetic	סוכרתי / סוכרתית sukrati **m** / sukratit **f**
I'm epileptic.	אני אפילפטי. / אני אפילפטית.
	ani epilepti. **m** / ani epileptit **f**
I'm allergic to	יש לי אלרגיה ל... yesh li alergya le...
antibiotics/	אנטיביוטיקה /פניצילין.
penicillin.	antibyotika/penitzilin.

I have...	...יש לי yesh li...
arthritis	דלקת מפרקים daleket mifrakim
a heart condition	בעיית לב be-ayat lev
high/low blood	לחץ דם גבוה/נמוך
pressure	lakhatz dam gavoha/namukh
I'm on...	...אני לוקח... / אני לוקחת
	ani loke-akh... m / ani lokakhat... f

For Meals & Cooking, see page 67.

162

YOU MAY HEAR...

מה קרה? ma kara?	What's wrong?
איפה כואב? eyfo ko-ev?	Where does it hurt?
האם כואב כאן? ha-im ko-ev kan?	Does it hurt here?
אתה לוקח תרופות? / את לוקחת תרופות?	Are you on medication?
ata loke-akh trufot? m/ at lokakhat trufot? f	
האם אתה אלרגי למשהו?	Are you allergic to
האם את אלרגית למשהו?	anything?
ha-im ata alergi lemashehu? m	
ha-im at alergit lemashehu? f	
פתח את הפה. / פתחי את הפה.	Open your mouth.
ptakh et hape. m / pitkhi et hape. f	
לנשום עמוק. תשתעל, בבקשה.	Breathe deeply.
לנשום עמוק. תשתעלי, בבקשה.	Cough, please.
linshom amok. tishta-el, bevakasha. m	
linshom amok. tishta-ali, bevakasha. f	
צריך ללכת לבית החולים.	Go to the hospital.
tzarikh lalekhet lebeyt hakholim.	

Treatment

Do I need a prescription/ medicine?	?האם אני צריך מרשם/תרופה ?האם אני צריכה מרשם/תרופה *ha-im ani tzarikh mirsham/trufa?* **m** *ha-im ani tzrikha mirsham/trufa?* **f**
Can you prescribe a generic drug?	?אפשר לרשום תרופה גנרית *efshar lirshom trufa generit?*
Where can I get it?	?איפה אפשר לקבל את זה *eyfo efshar lekabel et ze?*

For What to Take, see page 166.

Hospital

Notify my family, please.	.תודיעו למשפחה שלי, בבקשה *todi-u lamishpakha sheli, bevakasha*
I'm in pain.	.יש לי כאבים *yesh li ke'evim.*
I need a doctor/nurse.	אני צריך רופא/אחות. / אני צריכה רופא/אחות. *ani tzarikh rofe/akhot.* **m**/*ani tzrikha rofe akhot.* **f**
When are visiting hours?	?רופיבה תועש ןהמ *mahen sh-ot habikur?*
I'm visiting…	אני מבקר... / אני מבקרת... *ani mevaker…* **m** / *ani mevakeret…* **f**

Dentist

I have...	... יש לי *yesh li...*
a broken tooth	שן שבורה *shen shvura*
a lost filling	איבדתי סתימה *ibadeti stima*
a toothache	כאב שיניים *ke-ev shinayim*
Can you fix this denture?	?אפשר לתקן את השן התותבת *efshar letaken et hashen hatotevet?*

Gynecologist

I have cramps/ a vaginal infection.	אני סובלת מהתכווצויות/ זיהום נרתיקי. *ani sovelet mehitkavtzuyot/zihum nartiki.*
I missed my period.	המחזור שלי לא מגיע. *hamakhzor sheli lo magi-a.*
I'm on the Pill.	אני לוקחת גלולות נגד הריון. *ani lokakhat glulot neged herayon.*
I'm (...months) pregnant.	(...בהריון) אני *ani (beherayon...)* חודשים. *khodashim.*
I'm not pregnant.	אני לא בהריון. *ani lo beherayon.*
My last period was...	...המחזור האחרון שלי היה *hamakhzor ha-akharon sheli haya...*

For Numbers, see page 174.

Optician

I lost...	איבדתי... *ibadeti...*
a contact lens	עדשת מגע *adashat maga*
my glasses	את המשקפיים שלי *et hamishkafayim sheli*
a lens	עדשה *adasha*

Payment & Insurance

How much?	כמה זה עולה? *kama ze ole?*
Can I pay by credit card?	אפשר לשלם בכרטיס אשראי? *efshar leshalem bekartis ashray?*
I have insurance.	יש לי ביטוח. *yesh li bitu-akh.*
I need a receipt for my insurance.	אני צריך קבלה עבור הביטוח שלי. אני צריכה קבלה עבור הביטוח שלי. *ani tzarikh kabala avur habitu-akh sheli.* **m** *ani tzrikha kabala avur habitu-akh sheli.* **f**

Pharmacy

ESSENTIAL

Where's the pharmacy?	איפה בית המרקחת?
	eyfo beyt hamirkakhat?
What time does it open/close?	באיזה שעה זה נפתח/נסגר?
	be-eyze sha-a ze niftakh/nisgar?
What would you recommend for…?	על מה תמליץ בשביל…?
	על מה תמליצי בשביל…?
	al ma tamlitz bishvil…? **m**/ *al ma tamlitzi bishvil…?* **f**
How much do I take?	כמה צריך לקחת?
	kama tzarikh lakakhat?
I'm allergic to…	יש לי אלרגיה ל…
	yesh li alergya le…

In big cities, there are always plenty of pharmacies to choose from, some open 24-hours. The biggest issue is on Shabat, when everything is closed. However, there will be one open and on call in the area. Ask at your hotel or check a local newspaper for listings.

What to Take

How much do I take?	כמה צריך לקחת?
	kama tzarikh lakakhat?
How often?	באיזו תדירות?
	be-eyzo tadirut?
Is it safe for children?	האם זה בטוח לילדים?
	ha-im ze batu-akh liyeladim?

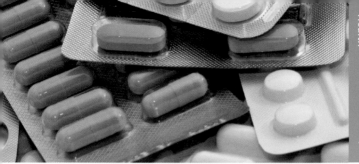

I'm taking...	אני לוקח... / אני לוקחת...	
	ani loke-akh... **m** */ ani lokakhat...* **f**	
Are there side effects?	האם יש תופעות לוואי?	
	ha-im yesh tofa-ot levay?	
I need something for...	אני צריך משהו ל... / אני צריכה משהו ל...	
	ani tzarikh mashehu le... **m** */ ani tzrikha mashehu le...* **f**	
a cold	הצטננות	*hitztanenut*
a cough	שיעול	*shi-ul*
diarrhea	שלשול	*shilshul*
a headache	כאב ראש	*ke-ev rosh*
insect bites	עקיצות חרקים	
	akitzot kharakim	
motion sickness	מחלת נסיעה	
	makhalat nesi-a	
a sore throat	כאב גרון	*ke-ev garon*
sunburn	כוויית שמש	
	kviyat shemesh	
a toothache	כאב שיניים	
	ke-ev shinayim	
an upset stomach	קלקול קיבה	
	kilkul keyva	

YOU MAY SEE...

פעם/שלוש פעמים ביום	once/three times a day
טבליה	tablet
טיפה	drop
כפית	teaspoon
...ארוחה	...meals
אחרי	after
לפני	before
עם	with
על קיבה ריקה	on an empty stomach
לבלוע שלם	swallow whole
עלול לגרום לעייפות	may cause drowsiness
לא לבלוע	do not ingest

Basic Supplies

I'd like...	אני רוצֶה... / אני רוצָה... ani rotze... **m** / ani rotza... **f**
acetaminophen [paracetamol]	אצטאמינופן atzetaminofen
antiseptic cream	משחה אנטיספטית mishkha antiseptit
aspirin	אספירין aspirin
Band-Aid [plasters]	פלסטרים plasterim
bandages	תחבושות takhboshot
a comb	קרסמ masrek
condoms	קונדומים kondomim
contact lens solution	תמיסה לעדשות מגע tmisa le-adashot maga

deodorant	דאודורנט *de-odorant*	
a hairbrush	מברשת לשיער *mivreshet lase-ar*	
hairspray	ספריי לשיער *sprey lase-ar*	
ibuprofen	איבופרופן *ibuprofen*	
insect repellent	דוחה חרקים *dokhe kharakim*	
lotion [moisturizing cream]	תחליב גוף *takhliv guf*	
a nail file	פצירת ציפורניים *ptzirat tzipornayim*	
a (disposable) razor	סכין גילוח (חד פעמי) *sakin gilu-akh (khad pe-ami)*	
razor blades	סכיני גילוח *sakiney gilu-akh*	
sanitary napkins [pads]	תחבושות היגייניות *takhboshot higiyeniyot*	
scissors	מספריים *misparayim*	
shampoo/ conditioner	שמפו/ מעצב שיער *shampo/ me-atzev se-ar*	
soap	סבון *sabon*	
sunscreen	קרם שיזוף (עם מקדם הגנה) *krem shizuf (im mekadem hagana)*	
tampons	טמפונים *tamponim*	
tissues	ממחטות נייר *mimkhatot neyar*	
toilet paper	נייר טואלט *neyar to-alet*	
toothpaste	משחת שיניים *mishkhat shinayim*	

For Baby Essentials, see page 149.

Grammar

Verbs

Verbs are generally shown in the dictionary in the infinitive with the
equivalent of **"to"** (**le-, la-,** or **li-**): **le-daber (to speak).** Different prefixes
and suffixes are added to **"a root"** to make the past, present, and future
forms. Although there are many variations, the following in the table below
are typical:

li-sigor (to close)		past	present	future
ani	I *m*	sagarti	soger	esgor
ani	I *f*	sagarti	sogeret	esgorl
ata	you *m*	sagarta	soger	tisgor
at	you *f*	sagart	sogeret	tisgeri
hu	he	sagar	soger	yisgor
hi	she	sagra	sogeret	tisgor
anakhnu	we *m*	sagarnu	sogrim	nisgor
anakhnu	we *f*	sagarnu	sogrot	nisgor
atem	you *m pl*	sagartem	sogrim	tisgeru
aten	you *f pl*	sagarten	sogrot	tisgorna
hem	they *m*	sagru	sogrim	yisgeru
hen	they *f*	sagru	sogrot	tisgorna

Nouns & Articles

Hebrew nouns belong to two genders: **masculine and feminine.**
Most feminine nouns end with the sound **"a"** *ah* , otherwise, they quite
obviously refer to feminine people (**em** – mother; **bat** – girl / daughter, etc.).

Ha, which is a prefix, means **"the"** and is used for both genders.
There is no equivalent of the English **"a/an"** or of the verb **"to be"** in
the present **(is/am/are).** This means you can have many sentences and
questions with no verb at all:

Example:

ani more.	I (am a) teacher.
eyfo habank?	Where (is) the bank?
kama ze?	How much (is) this?

Adjectives come after the noun. Those referring to feminine nouns also have to
be feminine and are usually formed by adding **a**:

khum	brown
sus khum	(a) brown horse
susa khuma	(a) brown mare

Adjectives referring to plural nouns have to agree with both the number and
the gender:

susim khumim	brown horses
susot khumot	brown mares

Nouns

Nouns are either masculine or feminine. It is not always easy to tell them
apart, but many feminine nouns end with **"a"** or refer to female people.
**Remember: the sentence changes slightly depending on whether you
are talking to a man or a woman.**

Indefinite & Definite Articles

There is no Hebrew equivalent of the English indefinite article **"a/ an".**

The definite article **ha-** (**the**) is used for both genders, in the singular and plural.

Examples:

Masculine	**ha-ish**	the man
Feminine	**ha-isha**	the woman
Masculine	**kise**	(a) chair
Feminine	**mita**	(a) bed

Plurals

Plurals are complicated and can sound significantly different from the singular. However, many masculine plurals are made by adding **–im** to the singular, and feminine plurals by adding **–ot**:

m	**bakbuk**	(a) bottle	**bakbukim**	bottles
f	**kos**	(a) glass	**kosot**	glasses

Adjectives

Adjectives come after the noun, and agree in gender and number. Adjectives are shown in the masculine singular. To make an adjective feminine, you usually add an **–a, -im** for masculine plural, and **–ot** for feminine plural. If the noun starts with ha-, then so should the adjective.

For example:

bakbuk gadol	(a) big bottle	**bakbukim gdolim**	big bottles
hakos hagdola	the big glass	**hakosot hagdolot**	the big glasses

Possessive Adjectives

To express possession (my, your, our, etc.) in Hebrew, you need to add a particular ending to the noun. For example:

khatul	cat	**khatuli**	my cat

my	**i**	**kahtuli**
your *m s*	**kha**	**khatulkha**

your *fs*	ekh	khatulekh
his	o	khatulo
her	a	khatula
our	enu	khatulenu
your	khem	khatulkhem
their	am	khatulam

You can also add the word **shel** (of) + an ending similar to the above:
e.g. **ha-khatul shelo** (the cat of his) = his cat

Questions

Questions are simple to form. There are two types:

1. Questions to which the answer is "yes" **(ken)** or "no" **(lo)**.
These are formed by simply raising the intonation at the end of a statement or by adding the question word **ha-im**:

| **Shimka Daveed.** | Your name is David. |
| **Shimka Daveed? / ha-im shimkha DavId?** | Is your name David? |

2. Other questions are formed by using the relevant question word:
Who? **Mi?**
Where? **Eyfo?**
What? **Ma?**
When? **Matay?**
Why? **Madua?**
How much/ many? **Kama?**
What's your name? **Ma shimka?**
When does the museum open? **Matay niftakh hamuze-on?**

Numbers

ESSENTIAL

0	אפס *efes*
1	אחד / אחת *ekhad* **m** / *akhat* **f**
2	שניים / שתיים *shnayim* **m** / *shtayim* **f**
3	שלושה / שלוש *shlosha* **m** / *shalosh* **f**
4	ארבעה / ארבע *arba-a* **m** / *arba* **f**
5	חמישה / חמש *khamisha* **m** / *khamesh* **f**
6	שישה / שש *shisha* **m** / *shesh* **f**
7	שבעה / שבע *shiv-a* **m** / *sheva* **f**
8	שמונה / שמונֶה *shmona* **m** / *shmone* **f**
9	תשעה / תשע *tish-a* **m** / *tesha* **f**
10	עשרה / עשר *asara* **m** / *eser* **f**
11	אחד עשר / אחת עשרה *ekhad asar* **m** / *akhat esre* **f**
12	שנים עשר / שתים עשרה *shnem asar* **m** / *shtem esre* **f**
13	שלושה עשר / שלוש עשרה *shlosha asar* **m** / *shlosh esre* **f**
14	ארבעה עשר / ארבע עשרה *arba-a asar* **m** / *arba esre* **f**
15	חמישה עשר / חמש עשרה *khamisha asar* **m** / *khamesh esre* **f**
16	שישה עשר / שש עשרה *shisha asar* **m** / *shesh esre* **f**
17	שבעה עשר / שבע עשרה *shiv-a asar* **m** / *shva esre* **f**
18	שמונה עשר / שמונֶה עשרה *shmona asar* **m** / *shmone esre* **f**

19	תשעה עשר / תשע עשרה
	tish-a asar [m / tsha esre f
20	עשרים *mirse*
21	עשרים ואחד / עשרים ואחת
	esrim ve-ekhad m / esrim ve-akhat f
22	עשרים ושניים / עשרים ושתיים
	esrim veshnayim m / esrim veshtayim f
30	שלושים *shloshim*
31	שלושים ואחד / שלושים ואחת
	shloshim ve-ekhad m / shloshim ve-akhat f
40	ארבעים *arba-im*
50	חמישים *khamishim*
60	שישים *shishim*
70	שבעים *shiv-im*
80	שמונים *shmonim*
90	תשעים *tish-im*
100	מאה *me-a*
101	מאה ואחד / מאה ואחת
	me-a ve-ekhad m / me-a ve-akhat f
200	מאתיים *matayim*
500	חמש מאות *khamesh me-ot*
1,000	אלף *elef*
10,000	עשרת אלפים *aseret alafim*
1,000,000	מיליון *milyon*

Ordinal Numbers

first	ראשון / ראשונה *rishon m / rishona f*
second	שני / שנייה *sheni m / shniya f*
third	שלישי / שלישית *shlishi m / shlishit f*
fourth	רביעי / רביעית *revi-i m / revi-it f*

fifth	חמישי / חמישית khamishi **f** / khamishit **f**
once	פעם אחת pa-am akhat
twice	פעמיים pa-amayim
three times	שלוש פעמים shalosh pe-amim

Time

ESSENTIAL

What time is it?	מה השעה? ma hasha-a?
It's midday.	צהריים עכשיו. tzohorayim akhshav.
At midnight.	בחצות הלילה. bekhatzot halayla.
From one o'clock to	מהשעה אחת עד השעה שתים.
two o'clock.	mehasha-a akhat ad hasha-a stayim.
Five past three.	שלוש וחמישה. shalosh vakhamisha.
A quarter to ten.	רבע לעשר. reva le-eser
5:30 a.m./p.m.	5:30 בבוקר/בערב.
	5:30 baboker/ba-erev.

Days

ESSENTIAL

Monday	יום שני yom sheni
Tuesday	יום שלישי yom shlishi
Wednesday	יום רביעי yom revi-i
Thursday	יום חמישי yom khamishi
Friday	יום שישי yom shishi
Saturday	יום שבת yom shabat
Sunday	יום ראשון yom rishon

Dates

Yesterday	אתמול	etmol
Today	היום	hayom
Tomorrow	מחר	makhar
Day	יום	yom
Week	שבוע	shavu-a
Month	חודש	khodesh
Year	שנה	shana
Happy New Year!	שנה חדשה שמחה!	shana khadasha smekha!
Happy Birthday!	יום הולדת שמח!	yom huledet same-akh!

Months

January	ינואר	yanu-ar
February	פברואר	febru-ar
March	מרץ	mertz
April	אפריל	april
May	מאי	may
June	יוני	Yuni
July	יולי	yuli
August	אוגוסט	ogust
September	ספטמבר	september
October	אוקטובר	october
November	נובמבר	november
December	דצמבר	detzember

Seasons

Spring	אביב	aviv
Summer	קיץ	kayitz
Autumn	סתיו	stav
Winter	חורף	khoref

Holidays (fixed)

January 1:	1 ביאנואר: יום השנה החדשה
New Year's Day	*1 beyanu-ar: yom hashana hakhadasha*
Holocaust Day	24th Nisan.
Memorial Day	4th Iyar
Independence Day	5th Iyar
May 1: Labor Day	1 במאי: יום העבודה
	1 bemay: yom ha-avoda
August 15:	15 באוגוסט חג עליית מרים לשמיים
Assumption Day	*15 be-ogust: khag aliyat miryam lashamayim*
November 1:	1בנובמבר: יום כל הקדושים
All Saints Day	*1 benovember: yom kol hakdoshim*
November 11:	11 בנובמבר: יום שביתת הנשק
Armistice Day	*11 benovember: yom shvitat haneshek*
December 25:	בדצמבר: חג המולד 25
Christmas	*25 be-detzember: khag hamolad*

Holidays (variable)

Good Friday	יום שישי הטוב *yom shishi hatov*
Easter	חג הפסחא *khag hapaskha*
Easter Monday	יום שני של חג הפסחא
	yom sheni shel khag hapaskha
Ascension	יום עלייתו של ישו לשמיים
	yom aliyato shel yeshu lashamayim
Eid al Adha	this is the beginning of Muslim Ramadan and follows a lunar calendar and drifts 11 days each year
Mohammed's Birthday	
Ramadan	one month of fasting from sunrise to sunset
Eid al Fitr	Conclusion of Ramadan, 3 day feast
Purim	15th of Hebrew month of Adar, (Adar Shani leap years)

Israel observes a solar-lunar year in accordance with Jewish religious tradition. As such, festival dates move each year. The Jewish New Year falls in September/ October with the festival of **Rosh Hashana**. The Muslim New Year is celebrated on 1 January.

Pesach – Passover	15th to 21 Nisan
Pentecost	תועובשה גח *khag hashavu-ot*
Jewish New Year	1st & 2nd Tishrei
Yom Kippur	10th Tishrei
Sukkot (Tabernacles)	15th to 23rd Tishrei
Hanukkah	25th to 3rd Tevet – festival of lights

Conversion Tables

When you know	Multiply by	To find
ounces	28.3	grams
pounds	0.45	kilograms
inches	2.54	centimeters
feet	0.3	meters
miles	1.61	kilometers
square inches	6.45	sq. centimeters
square feet	0.09	sq. meters
square miles	2.59	sq. kilometers
pints (U.S./Brit)	0.47/0.56	liters
gallons (U.S./Brit)	3.8/4.5	liters
Fahrenheit	-32, / 1.8	Centigrade
Centigrade	+32 , x 1.8	Fahrenheit

Kilometers to Miles Conversions

1 km	=	0.62 miles
20 km	=	12.4 miles
5 km	=	3.1 miles
50 km	=	31 miles
100 km	=	62 miles

Measurement

1 gram	= **1000 milligrams**	= 0.035 oz.
1 kilogram (kg)	= **1000 grams**	= 2.2 lb
1 liter (l)	= **1000 milliliters**	= 1.06 U.S./0.88
1 centimeter	= **10 millimeters**	= 0.4 inch (cm)
1 meter (m)	= **100 centimeters**	= 39.37 inches/ 3.28 ft.
1 kilometer	= **1000 meters**	= 0.62 mile (km)

Temperature

-40°C = -40°F	**-1°C** = 30°F	**20°C** = 68°F
-30°C = -22°F	**0°C** = 32°F	**25°C** = 77°F
-20°C = -4°F	**5°C** = 41°F	**30°C** = 86°F
-10°C = 14°F	**10°C** = 50°F	**35°C** = 95°F
-5°C = 23°F	**15°C** = 59°F	

Oven Temperature

100° C = 212° F	**177° C** = 350° F
121° C = 250° F	**204° C** = 400° F
149° C = 300° F	**260° C** = 500° F

... תודיע לי... מכתב todi-a li, mikhtav 152; **~box** תיבת דואר tevat do-ar
...evel (adj.) ישר yashar 31
...rary ספריה sifriya
to ~ down לשכב lishkav 164
~belt חגורת הצלה khagorat
...ala: **~boat** סירת הצלה sirat
...la: **~guard** מציל הצלה matzil 116; חגורת הצלה khagorat
... ma-alit 26, 132;
...ng) טרמפ tremp 83
...or 25; (bicycle) אור
...; (weight) קל kal 14, בהיר bahir 14, 134, 143; יותר yoter bahir 143
...nura 148
... מצית matzit 150
...hev 119, 121, 125; זה ze motze

lobby (theater, hote... אולם כניסה ulam knisa
local מקומי mekom...
lock (noun) מנעול
lock, to לנעול lin-ol 8...
myself out of my roo... את עצמי מחוץ לחדר atzmi mikhutz lakhede...
log on, to להתחבר lehitk...
long ארוך arokh 144, 146
long-distance bus אוטובוס otobus beyn-ironi 77
look: to ~ for לחפש lekhape...
I'm looking for ... מחפש mekhapes 143; to ~ like lehera-ot 71; I'm just looking אני רק מסתכל ani rak mistake...
loose חופשי khofshi 146
lorry משאית
lose, to

English – Hebrew

Hebrew Alphabet		khet	ח	ayin	ע
alef	א	tet	ט	pe	פ
bet	ב	yod	י	tzadi	צ
gimel	ג	kaf	כ	kof	ק
dalet	ד	lamed	ל	resh	ר
heh	ה	mem	מ	shin	ש
vav	ו	nun	נ	tav	ת
zayin	ז	samekh	ס		

A

able יכול / יכולה
  yakhol (m) / yekhola (f)

about לגבי *legabey*

above מעל *me-al*

accept v (approval) לקבל
  lekabel

access n גישה *gisha*

accessory אביזר *avizar*

accident תאונה *te-unah*

account חשבון
  kheshbon

ache כאב *ke-ev*

acupuncture טיפול בדיקור
  tipul Bedikur

adapter מתאם *mat-em*

address n כתובת *ktovet*

admission כניסה *knisah*

admitted אושפז *ushpaz*

after לאחר *le-akhar*

afternoon אחר הצהרים
  akhar hatzohorayim

again שוב *shuv*

against נגד *neged*

age גיל *gil*

air conditioning מיזוג אוויר
  mizug avir

air mattress מזרן אוויר
  mizran avir

airmail דואר אוויר
  do-ar avir

airplane מטוס *matos*

airport שדה תעופה
  sdeh te-ufa

aisle seat מושב ליד המעבר
  moshav leyad ha-ma-avar

alarm clock שעון מעורר
  sha-on me-orer

alcohol אלכוהול *alkohol*

alcoholic *adj* אלכוהולי *alkoholi*

allergic אלרגית / אלרגי
alergi (m) / alergit (f)

allergic reaction תגובה אלרגית
tguva alerqit

alphabet אלף-בית *alef-bet*

also כמו כן *kmo khen*

alter *v* לשנות *leshanot*

altitude sickness מחלת גבהים
makhalat gvahim

amazing מדהים *madhim*

amber ענבר *inbar*

ambulance אמבולנס
ambulance

American
אמריקאי / אמריקאית
amerika-i (m) / amerika-it (f)

amethyst אחלמה *akhlama*

amount *n* **(money)** סכום
skhum

amusement park
פארק שעשועים
park sha-ashu-im

analgesic משכך כאבים
meshakekh ke-evim

and ו *ve*

anesthetic חומר מרדים
khomer mardim

animal בעל חיים
ba-al kha-im

ankle קרסול *karsol*

answer תשובה *tshuva*

antibiotic אנטיביוטיקה *antibyotika*

antidepressant נוגד דיכאון
noged dika-on

antique עתיק *atik*

antiques store חנות עתיקות
khanut atikot

antiseptic cream
משחה לחיטוא
mishkha lekhitu

any כלשהו / כלשהי
kolshehu (m) / kolshehi (f)

anyone כל אחד / כלאחאת
kol ekhad (m) / kol akhat (f)

anything כל דבר שהוא
kol davarshehu

anywhere כל מקום שהוא
kol makom shehu

apartment דירה *dirah*

aperitif אפריטיף *aperitif*

appendix תוספתן *tosaftan*

appliance מוצר חשמלי
mutzar khashmali

appointment פגישה *pgisha*

arcade ארקדה *arkada*

architect ארכיטקט / ארכיטקטית
arkhitekt (m) / arkhitektit (f)

arm זרוע *zro-a*

aromatherapy ארומתרפיה
aromaterapya

**around (approximately)
; (around the corner)**
מעבר me-ever

arrival הגעה haga-a

arrive להגיע lehagi-a

art אמנות amanut

art gallery גלריית אמנות
galeryat amanot

aspirin אספירין aspirin

assistance סיוע siyu-a

assorted מגוון migvan

asthma אסתמה astma

astringent
חומר עוצר דימום
khomer otzer dimum

at ב be

ATM כספומט kaspomat

attack n התקפה hatkafa

attend להשתתף
lehishtatef

attractive מושך / מושכת
moshekh (m) / moshekhet (f)

audio guide מדריך קולי
madrikh koli

Australia אוסטרליה ostralya

average ממוצע memutza

away הרחק harkhek

awful נורא nora

B

baby תינוק / תינוקת
tinok (m) / tinoket (f)

baby bottle בקבוק לתינוק
bakbuk latinok

baby food אוכל תינוקות
okhel tinokot

baby wipes מגבונים לתינוק
magvonim latinok

babysitter בייביסיטר
baybisiter

back v לחזור lakhazor; n גב gav

backache כאב גב ke-ev gav

backpack תרמיל גב
tarmil gav

bad רע / רעה
ra (m) / ra-a (f)

**bag (purse/ [handbag])
; (shopping)** תיק tik

baggage [BE] מטען mitan

baggage check בדיקת מטען
bdikat mitan

baggage claim קבלת מזוודות
kabalat mizvadot

bakery מאפיה ma-afiya

balance (finance) יתרה yitra

balcony מרפסת mirpeset

ballet בלט balet

bandage n תחבושת
takhboshet

bank (finance) בנק bank

bank note שטר כסף
shtar kesef

bar בר bar

barber ספר *sefer*

basket סל *sal*

basketball game משחק כדורסל
  miskhak kadursal

bath אמבטיה *ambatya*

bathing suit בגד ים *beged yam*

bathrobe חלוק רחצה
  khaluk rakhatza

bathroom שירותים *sherutim*

battery סוללה *solela*

battleground שדה קרב
  sdeh krav

be להיות *lihiyot*

beach ball כדור חוף
  kadur khof

beard זקן *zakan*

beautiful יפה
  yafe (m) / yafa (f)

beauty salon מכון יופי
  makhon yofi

bed מיטה *mita*

before (time) לפני *lifney*

begin להתחיל *lehatkhil*

behind מאחור *me-akhor*

beige בז' *bezh*

bell (electric) פעמון *pa-amon*

below מתחת *mitakhat*

belt חגורה *khagora*

berth הניש שגרד *dargash she-na*

better יותר טוב *yoter tov*

between בין *beyn*

bicycle אופניים *ofana-im*

big גדול / גדולה
  gadol (m) / gdola (f)

bike route נתיב אופניים
  netiv ofana-im

bikini ביקיני *bikini*

**bill (restaurant)
  ; (bank note)** חשבון
  kheshbon

binoculars משקפת *mishkefet*

bird ציפור *tzipor*

birth לידה *leyda*

birthday יום הולדת
  yom huledet

black שחור *shakhor*

bladder שלפוחית *shalpukhit*

blade להב *lahav*

blanket שמיכה *smikha*

bleach מלבין *malbin*

bleed לדמם *ledamem*

blind (window) תריס *tris*

blister אבעבועה *ava-abuah*

blocked חסום / חסומה
  khasum (m) / khasuma (f)

blood דם *dam*

blood pressure לחץ דם
  lakhatz dam

blouse חולצה *khultza*

blow dry לעשות פן
  la-asot fen

blue כחול *kakhol*

boat סירה *sira*

boat trip יציאה להפלגה *yetziah lehaflaga*

body גוף *guf*

bone עצם *etzem*

book ספר *sefer*

booklet (of tickets) חוברת *khoveret*

bookstore חנות ספרים *khanut sfarim*

boot מגף *magaf*

boring משעמם *mesha-amem*

born נולד / נולדה *nolad (m) / nolda (f)*

botanical garden גן בוטני *gan botani*

botany בוטניקה *botanika*

bother לטרוח *litro-akh*

bottle בקבוק *bakbuk*

bottle opener פותחן בקבוקים *potkhan bakbukim*

bottom תחתית *takhtit*

bowel מעי *me-i*

bowl קערה *ke-ara*

box קופסה *kufsa*

boxing match תחרות אגרוף *takharut igruf*

boy ילד *yeled*

boyfriend חבר *khaver*

bra חזיה *khaziya*

bracelet צמיד *tzamid*

brake *n* בלם *balam*

break (out of order) התקלקל *hitkalkel*

breakdown (car) התקלקלה *hitkalkela*

breakfast ארוחת בוקר *arukhat Boker*

breast חזה *khazeh*

breathe לנשום *linshom*

bridge גשר *gesher*

bring להביא *lehavi*

bring down להוריד *lehorid*

British (person) בריטי / בריטית *briti (m) / britit (f)*

broken שבור / שבורה *shavur (m) / shvura (f)*

brooch סיכת נוי לבגד *sikat noy labeged*

broom מטאטא *matate*

brown חום *khum*

bruise חבורה *khavura*

brush *n* מברשת *mivreshet*

bucket דלי *dli*

bug חרק *kherek*

build לבנות *livnot*

building בניין *binyan*

burn לשרוף *lisrof*

bus אוטובוס *otobus*

bus station תחנת אוטובוס *takhanat otobus*

bus stop תחנת אוטובוס

takhanat otobus

business card כרטיס ביקור
kartis bikur

business center (at hotel)
מרכז עסקים *merkaz asakim*

business class מחלקת עסקים
makhleket asakim

business district מחוז עסקים
makhoz asakim

business trip נסיעת עסקים
nesi-at asakim

busy עסוק / עסוקה
asuk (m) / asuka (f)

but אבל *aval*

butane gas גז בוטן
gaz butan

butcher קצב *katzav*

button כפתור *kaftor*

buy לקנות *liknot*

C

cabin (ship) תא *ta*

cafe בית קפה *beyt kafe*

calculator מחשבון
makhshevon

calendar לוח שנה *lu-akh shana*

call n (phone) שיחה; **v; (summon)**
לקרוא *sikha likro*

calm רגוע / רגועה
ragu-a (m) / regu-a (f)

camera מצלמה *matzlema*

camera case תיק למצלמה

tik lematzlema

camera shop חנות למצלמות
khanut lematzlemot

camp bed מיטת מחנה
mitat makhane

camp v להקים מחנה
lehakim makhane

camping מחנאות
makhana-ut

camping equipment ציוד למחנאות
tziud lemakhana-ut

campsite אתר מחנאות
atar makhana-ut

can opener פותחן *potkhan*

can v (be able to) יכול / יכולה
yakhol (m) / yekhola (f);
n (container) פחית שימורים *pakhit
shimurim "*

Canada קנדה *kanada*

Canadian קנדי / קנדית
kanadi (m) / kanadit (f)

cancel לבטל *levatel*

candle נר *ner*

candy store חנות ממתקים
khanut mamtakim

cap מכסה *mikhse*

car מכונית *mekhonit*

car hire [BE] השכרת רכב
haskarat rekhev

car mechanic מכונאי רכב
mekhona-i rekhev

car park [BE] מגרש חניה
migrash khanaya

car rental השכרת רכב
haskarat rekhev

car seat מושב מכונית
moshav mekhonit

carafe קנקן *kankan*

card (Greeting) כרטיס (ברכה) *kartis
(brakha)*; **(game)** קלף *; klaf*

card game משחק קלפים
miskhak klafim

cardigan קרדיגן *kardigan*

carry לשאת *laset*

cart עגלה *agala*

carton (of cigarettes) קרטון
karton

case (camera) תיק *tik*

cash v לפדות; n כסף מזומן *lifdot ; kesef mezuman*

cashier קופאי / קופאית
kupa-i (m) / kupa-it (f)

casino קזינו *kazino*

castle slot; טירה *tira*

caution זהירות *zehirut*

cave מערה *me-ara*

CD תקליטור *taklitor*

cell phone טלפון סלולרי
telefon selolari

cemetery בית קברות
beyt kvarot

center of town מרכז העיר

merkaz ha-ir

centimeter סנטימטר *sentimeter*

ceramics קרמיקה *keramika*

certain בטוח / בטוחה
batu'akh (m) / betukha (f)

certificate תעודה *te-uda*

chair כסא *kise*

change n עודף *odef* **(money)** ; v
לפרוט *lifrot* **(money)**;
v **(clothes, diaper)**
להחליף *lehakhlif*

charcoal פחם *pekham*

charge n; חיוב *khiyuv*; v לחייב;
lekhayev

cheap זול *zol*

check (restaurant)
n חשבון *kheshbon*;
(banking) המחאה *hamkha-ah*;
v **(someone, something)**
לבדוק *livdok*

check-in desk (airport)
דלפק צ׳ק-אין *dalpak chek-in*

checking account
חשבון עובר ושב
kheshbon over vashav

check out v לעשות צ׳ק אאוט
la-asot chek awt

check-up (medical) בדיקה
bdika

cheers לחיים *lekha-im*

chef שף *shef*

chemical toilet
בית שימוש כימי
beyt shimush khimi

chemist [BE] כימאי / כימאית
khima-i (m) / khima-it (f)

cheque [BE] המחאה
hmkha-ah

chess שחמט shakhmat

chess set ערכת שחמט
erkat shakhmat

chest חזה khaze

chest pain כאבים בחזה
ke-evim bakhaze

child ילד / ילדה
yeled (m) / yalda (f)

child's seat מושב לילד
moshav layeled

children's clothing בגדי ילדים
bigdey yeladim

children's portion מנה לילדים
mana liyeladim

choice בחירה bkhira

church כנסיה knesiya

cigar סיגר sigar

cigarette סיגריה sigarya

cinema [BE] קולנוע kolnoa

classical קלאסי klasi

clean adj; נקי / נקיה naki (m)/nekiya(f)
נלקות lenakot

cleansing cream קרם ניקוי
krem nikuy

clear v לפנות lefanot

cliff צוק tzuk

clip לחתוך lakhtokh

clock שעון sha-on

close v לסגור lisgor

closed סגור sagur

cloth מטלית matlit

clothing ביגוד bigud

clothing store חנות בגדים
khanut bgadim

cloud ענן anan

coat n (**clothing**) מעיל me-il

coin מטבע matbe-a

cold (illness); הצטננות hitztanenut ;
adj קר kar

collar צווארון tzavaron

colleague עמית / עמיתה
amit (m) / amita (f)

color צבע tzeva

comb מסרק masrek

come לבוא lavo

comedy קומדיה komedya

commission (fee) עמלה amla

common (frequent) נפוץ
nafotz

compartment (train) תא ta

compass מצפן matzpen

complaint תלונה tluna

computer (PC) מחשב
makhshev

concert הופעה hofa-a

concert hall אולם קונצרטים
ulam kontzertim

condom קונדום *kondom*

conference room חדר וועידה
kheder ve-ida

confirm לאשר *le-asher*

confirmation אישור *ishur*

congratulations מזל טוב
mazal tov

connect v לחבר *lekhaber*

connection (transportation, internet) חיבור *khibur*

constipation עצירות *atzirut*

consulate קונסוליה *konsulya*

contact lens עדשות מגע
adashot maga

contagious מדבק *medabek*

contain מכיל / מכילה
mekhil (m) /mekhila (f)

contraceptive אמצעי מניעה
emtza-i meni-ah

contract חוזה *khoze*

control שליטה *shlita*

convention hall מרכז וועידות
merkaz ve-idot

cooking facilities מתקני בישול
mitkaney bishul

copper נחושת *nekhoshet*

corkscrew חולץ פקקים
kholetz pkakim

corner פינ *pina*

cost n עלות *alut;*
v לעלות *a-alot*

cot מיטה מתקפלת
mita mitkapelet

cotton כותנה *kutna*

cough n שיעול *shi-ul*

counter דלפק *dalpak*

country מדינה *medina*

countryside כפר *kfar*

court house בית המשפט
beyt hamishpat

cover charge דמי כניסה
dmey knisah

cramps עווית *avit*

crayon צבעון *tzivon*

cream (toiletry) קרם *krem*

credit אשראי *ashray*

credit card כרטיס אשראי
kartis ashray

crib עריסה *arisa*

crockery [BE] כלי חרס
kli kheres

cross-country skiing סקי למרחקים
ski lemerkhakim

crossing (maritime) חצייה*khatzaya*

crossroads צמתים *tzmatim*

crown (Danish currency) קרונה
karona

crystal בדולח *bdolakh*

cufflink חפת *khefet*

cuisine מטבח *mitbakh*

cup ספל *sefel*

currency מטבע *matbe-a*

currency exchange office
משרד לחילופי מט"ח
misrad lekhilufey matakh

current (ocean) זרם *zerem*

curtain וילון *vilon*

customs מכס *mekhes*

customs declaration form
טופס הצהרת מכס
tofes hatzharat mekhes

cut n (wound) חתך *khatakh*;
v (with scissors) לגזור *ligzor*

cut glass זכוכית מלוטשת
zkhukhit meluteshet

cycling race מרוץ אופניים
merotz ofanayim

D

dairy מוצרי חלב
mutzarey khalav

damaged פגום / פגומה
pagum (m) / pguma (f)

dance club מועדון לילה
mo-adon layla

dance n ריקוד *rikud*;
v לרקוד *lirkod*

danger סכנה *sakana*

dangerous מסוכן *mesukan*

Danish (person); adj דני / דנית
deni (m) / denit (f)

dark חשוך *khashukh*

date (appointment) פגישה *pgisha*;
(day) תאריך *ta-arikh*

day יום *yom*

decision החלטה *hakhlata*

deck (ship) סיפון *sipun*

deck chair כסא נוח *kisse no-akh*

declare (customs) להצהיר
lehatzhir

deep עמוק *amok*

degree (temperature) מעלה
ma-ala

delay עיכוב *ikuv*

delicatessen מעדניה
ma-adaniya

delicious טעים *ta-im*

deliver להביא *lehavi*

delivery משלוח *mishlo-akh*

denim ג'ינס *Jlns*

Denmark דנמרק
denemark

dentist רופא שיניים
rofe shinayim

denture שן תותבת
shen totevet

deodorant דיאודורנט
de-odorant

depart לעזוב *la-azov*

department (shop) מחלקה
makhlaka

department store חנות כלבו
khanut Kolbo

departure עזיבה *aziva*

departure gate שער יציאה
sha-ar yetziah

**deposit n (bank);
(down payment)** הפקדה *hafkada*

dessert קינוח *kinu-akh*

detergent חומר ניקוי
khomer nikuy

detour (traffic) מעקף
ma-akaf

diabetic סוכרתי / סוכרתית
sukrati (m) / sukratit (f)

diamond יהלום
yahalom

diaper חיתול *khitul*

diarrhea שלשול *shilshul*

dictionary מילון *milon*

diesel דיזל *dizel*

diet דיאטה *dyeta*

difficult קשֶה / קשה
kashe (m) / kasha (f)

digital דיגיטאלי / דיגיטאלית
digitali (m) / digitalit (f)

dining car קרון מסעדה
karon misada

dining room חדר אוכל
kheder okhel

dinner ארוחת ערב
arukhat erev

direct adj ; v (someone)
ישיר לכוון *yashir lekhaven*

direction כיווּן *kivun*

directory (phone) מדריך
madrikh

dirty מלוכלך / מלוכלכת
melukhlakh (m) / melukhlekhet (f)

disabled נכֶה / נכה
nekhe (m) / nekkha (f)

disc (parking) תו (חניה)
tav (khanaya)

disconnect v (computer)
להתנתק *lehitnatek*

discount הנחה *hanakha*

disease מחלה
makhala

dish (food item) מאכל
ma-akhal

dishes (plates) כלים *kelim*

dishwasher מדיח כלים
medi-akh kelim

dishwashing detergent
חומר ניקוי למדיח כלים
khomer nikuy lemedi-akh kelim

disinfectant חומר מחטא
khomer mekhate

display case תיבת תצוגה
teyvat tetzuga

district (of town) רובע *rova*

disturb להפריע
lehafri-a

divorced גרוש / גרושה
garush (m) / grusha (f)

dizzy /סובל מסחרחורת
סובלת מסחרחורת
sovel miskharkhoret (m) /
sovelet miskharkhoret (f)

doctor רופא / רופאה
rofe (m) / rofa (f)

doctor's office מרפאה
mirpa-ah

dog כלב *kelev*

doll בובה *buba*

dollar (U.S.) דולר *dolar*

domestic (airport terminal)
פנים ארצי *pnim artzi*

domestic flight טיסה פנים-ארצית
tisa pnim artzit

double bed מיטה כפולה
mita kfula

double room חדר כפול
kheder kaful

down למטה *lemata*

downtown area
אזור העיר התחתית
ezor ha-ir hatakhtit

dozen תריסר *treysar*

dress *n* שמלה *simla*

drink *n* ; (cocktail);
משקה לשתות *v*
mashke lishtot

drinking water מי שתיה
mey shtiya

drip טפטוף *tiftuf*

drive לנהוג *linhog*

driver's license רשיון נהיגה
rishyon nehiga

drop (liquid) טיפה *tipa*

drugstore בית מרקחת
beyt merkakhat

dry יבש / יבשה
yavesh (m) / yevesha (f)

dry cleaner ניקוי יבש
nikuy yavesh

dummy [BE] (baby's) מוצץ
motzetz

during במשך *bemeshekh*

duty (customs) מס *mas*

duty-free goods
מוצרים פטורים ממכס
mutzarim pturim mimekhes

duty-free shop חנות דיוטי-פרי
khanut dyuti fri

dye עבצ *tzeva*

E

each כל אחד *kol ekhad*

ear אוזן *ozen*

ear drops
טיפות אוזניים
tipot oznayim

earache כאב אוזניים
ke-ev oznayim

early מוקדם *mukdam*

earring עגיל *agil*

east מזרח *mizrakh*

easy קל *kal*

eat לאכול *le-ekhol*

economy class מחלקת תיירים *makhleket tayarim*

elastic אלסטי *elasti*

electric חשמלי *khashmali*

electrical outlet שקע חשמלי *sheka khashmali*

electricity חשמל *kashmal*

electronic אלקטרוני *elektroni*

elevator מעלית *ma-alit*

e-mail האימייל *haemail*

e-mail address כתובת האימייל *ktovet haemail*

embassy שגרירות *shagrirut*

embroidery ריקמה *rikma*

emerald אזמרגד *izmargad*

emergency חירום *kherum*

emergency exit
יציאת חירום
yetziat kherum

empty ריק *rek*

enamel תזגיג *tazgig*

end לסיים *lesayem*

engaged (phone) תפו *tafus*

England אנגליה *anglia*

English (language) אנגלית *anglit*;
(person) אנגלי / אנגליה
angli (m) / anglia (f)

enjoyable מהנה *mehane*

enlarge להגדיל *lehagdil*

enough מספיק *maspik*

enter v **enter somewhere** ;
enter IT content להיכנס / להכניס
lehikanes; lehakhnis

entrance כניסה *knisa*

entrance fee דמי כניסה
dmey knisa

entry (access) רשומה *reshuma*

envelope מעטפה *ma-atafa*

equipment ציוד *tziyud*

eraser מחק *makhak*

escalator מעלית *ma-alit*

estimate n ; **(quotation)**
הצעת מחיר *hatza-at mekhir*

e-ticket כרטיס אלקטרוני
kartis elektroni

e-ticket check-in
צ'ק-אין עם כרטיס אלקטרוני
chek in im kartis elektroni

Europe אירופה *eyropa*

European Union
האיחוד האירופי
ha-ikhud ha-eyropi

evening ערב *erev*

every כל *kol*

everything הכל *hakol*

exchange rate שער החליפין
sha-ar hakhalifin

exchange v **(money)** להמיר
lehamir

excursion טיול *tiyul*

excuse v לתרץ *letaretz*

exhibition תערוכה *ta-arukha*

exit n ; v (computer)
יציאה לצאת
yetziah latzet

expect לצפות *litzpot*

expense הוצאה *hotza-a*

expensive יקר *yakar*

express לבטא *levate*

expression ביטוי *bituy*

extension (phone) שלוחה
shlukha

extra אקסטרה *extra*

eye עין *ayln*

eye drops טיפות עיניים
tipot eynayim

eye shadow צללית לעין
tzlalit la-ayin

eyesight ראיה *re-iya*

F

fabric (cloth) בד *bad*

face פנים *panim*

facial טיפול פנים *tipul panim*

factory מפעל *mifal*

fair הוגן / הוגנת
hogen (m) / hogenet (f)

fall v ליפול *lipol*

family משפחה *mishpakha*

fan (device); (person)
הציריעם / צירעם ררוואם *me-avrer;*
ma-aritz (m) / ma-aritza (f)

far רחוק / רחוקה
rakhok (m) / rekhoka (f)

fare (ticket) דמי נסיעה
dmey nesi-a

farm הווה *khava*

far-sighted רחוק רואי
rekhok ro-i

fast adj מהיר / מהירה
mahir (m) / mehira (f)

fast-food place מסעדת מזון מהיר
misedet mazon mahir

faucet ברז *berez*

fax פקס *fax*

fax number מספר פקס
mispar faks

fee (commission) עמלה *amla*

feed v להאכיל *leha-akhil*

feel (physical state) להרגיש
lehargish

ferry מעבורת *ma-aboret*

fever חום *khom*

few קומץ *kometz*

field שדה *sade*

file (for nails) פצירה *ptzira*

fill in (form) למלא *lemale*

filling (tooth) סתימה *stima*

film [BE] (v); (n) להסריט; סרט
lehasrit; seret

filter מסנן *mesanen*

find v למצוא *limtzo*

fine (OK) בסדר *beseder*

fine arts אמנויות יפות
omanuyot yafot

finger אצבע *etzba*

fire אש *esh*

fire door דלת חסינת אש
delet khasinat esh

fire escape יציאת חירום
yetziat kherum

fire exit יציאת חירום
yetziat kherum

first ראשון / ראשונה
rishon (m) / rishona (f)

first-aid kit ערכת עזרה ראשונה
erkat ezra rishona

first class מחלקה ראשונה
makhlaka rishona

first course מנה ראשונה
mana rishona

fishing דייג *dayig*

fit v להתאים *lehat-im*

fitting room חדר מדידה
kheder medida

fix v לתקן *letaken*

flashlight פנס *panas*

flat [BE] (apartment) דירה *dira*

flatware כלי אוכל *kley okhel*

flea market שוק הפשפשים
shuk hapishpeshim

flight טיסה *tisa*

floor רצפה *ritzpa*

florist חנות פרחים

khanut prakhim

flower פרח *perakh*

flu שפעת *shapa-at*

fluid נוזל *nozel*

fog ערפל *arafel*

follow לעקוב *la-akov*

food אוכל *okhel*

food poisoning הרעלת מזון
haralat mazon

foot כף רגל *kaf regel*

football [BE] כדורגל *kaduregel*

for עבור *avur*

forbidden אסור *asur*

forecast תחזית *takhazit*

foreign זר *zar*

forest יער *ya-ar*

forget לשכוח *lishko-akh*

fork מזלג *mazleg*

form (document) טופס *tofes*

fountain (body of water) מעין
ma'ayan

(drinking facility)
מעין *birziya*

frame (glasses) מסגרת
misgeret

free בחינם *bekhinam*

freezer מקפיא *makpi*

fresh טרי *tari*

friend חבר / חברה
khaver (m) / khavera (f)

from מאת *me-et*

frost כפור *kfor*

frying pan מחבת לטיגון *makhvat letigun*

full מלא *male*

full-time במשרה מלאה *bemisra belea*

furniture ריהוט *rihut*

G

gallery גלריה *galeria*

game משחק *miskhak*

garage חניה מקורה *khanaya mekura*

garbage זבל *zevel*

garden גינה *gina*

gas דלק *delek*

gasoline דלק *delek*

gauze גאזה *gaza*

gem אבן חן *even khen*

general כללי *klali*

general delivery משלוח כללי *mishlo-akh klali*

general practitioner [BE] רופא משפחה *rofe mishpakha*

genuine מקורי *mekori*

get (find) להשיג *lehasig*

get off לרדת *laredet*

get up לעלות *la-alot*

gift מתנה *matana*

gift shop חנות מתנות *khanut matanot*

girl ילדה *yalda*

girlfriend חברה *khavera*

give לתת *latet*

gland בלוטה *baluta*

glass (drinking) כוס *kos*

glasses (optical) משקפיים *mishkafa-im*

glove כפפה *kfafa*

glue דבק *devek*

go away לעזוב *la-azov*

go back לחזור *lakhazor*

go out לצאת *latzet*

gold זהב *zahav*

golf club מועדון גולף *mo-adon golf*

golf course מגרש גולף *migrash golf*

golf tournament טורניר גולף *turnir golf*

good טוב / טובה *tov (m) / tova (f)*

good afternoon אחר צהריים טובים *akhar tzohora-im Tovim*

good evening ערב טוב *erev tov*

good morning בוקר טוב *boker tov*

good night לילה טוב *layla tov*

goodbye להתראות *lehitra-ot*

gram גרם *gram*

grandchild נכד *nekhed*

gray אפור *afor*

great (excellent) נהדר *nehedar*

Great Britain בריטניה *britanya*

green ירוק *yarok*

greengrocer's [BE] ירקן *yarkan*

greeting ברכה *brakha*

ground-floor room [BE]
חדר בקומת קרקע
kheder bekomat karka

groundsheet יריעת קרקע
yeri-at karka

group קבוצה *kvutza*

guesthouse בית הארחה
beyt ha-arakha

guide dog כלב נחיה
kelev nekhiya

guide *n* מדריך / מדריכה
madrikh (m) / madrikha (f)

guidebook מדריך טיולים
madrikh tiyulim

gym חדר כושר *kheder kosher*

gynecologist
רופא נשים / רופאת נשים
rofe nashim (m) / rofat nashim (f)

H

hair שיער *se-ar*

hair dryer מייבש שיער
meyabesh Se-ar

hairbrush מברשת לשיער
mivreshet Lase-ar

haircut תספורת *tisporet*

hairdresser ספר / ספרית
sapar (m) / saparit (f)

hairspray ספריי לשיער
sprey lase-ar

hall (room) אולם *ulam*

hammer פטיש *patish*

hammock ערסל *arsal*

hand יד *yad*

hand cream קרם לידיים
krem Layadayim

hand washable לרחיצה ביד
lirkhitza Bayad

handbag [BE] תיק *tik*

handicrafts מלאכת יד
melekhet yad

handkerchief מטפחת
mitpakhat

handmade תוצרת יד
totzeret yad

hanger קולב *kolav*

happy שמח / שמחה
same-akh (m) / smekha (f)

harbor נמל *namal*

hard קשה *kashe*

hardware store חנות לחומרי בניין
khanut lekhomrey binyan

hare ארנבת *arnevet*

hat כובע *kova*

have (must) חייב *khayav*;

have (possess)
יש *yesh*

hay fever קדחת השחת
kadakhat hashakhat

head ראש *rosh*

headache כאב ראש *ke-ev rosh*

headlight פנס קדמי *panas kidmi*

headphones אוזניות *ozniyot*

health food store
חנות טבע *khanut teva*

health insurance ביטוח בריאות
bitu-akhbri-ut

hearing-impaired
לקוי שמיעה / לקויית שמיעה
lekuy shmi-a (m) /
lekuyat Shmi-a (f)

heart לב *lev*

heart attack התקוף לב *hetkef lev*

heat v לחמם *lekhamem*

heating חימום *khimum*

heavy כבד / כבדה
kaved (m) / kveda (f)

hello שלום *shalom*

helmet קסדה *kasda*

help; (oneself) לעזור *la-azor*

here כאן **kan**

hi שלום **shalom**

high adj גבוה / גבוהה
gavo-a (m) / gvoha (f)

high tide גאות *ge-ut*

highchair כיסא האכלה
kise ha'akhala

highway כביש מהיר
kvish mahir

hill גבעה *giv-a*

hire [BE] v להעסיק *leha-asik*

history היסטוריה *historya*

hole חור *khor*

holiday; [BE] [vacation] חופשה
khufsha

home בית *bayit*

horseback riding
רכיבה על סוסים
rekhiva al susim

hospital בית חולים *beyt kholim*

hot (temperature) חם *kham*

hotel בית מלון *beyt malon*

hotel directory מדריך מלונות
madrikh melonot

hotel reservation הזמנה למלון
hazmana lemalon

hour (time) שעה *sha'a*

house בית *bayit*

how איך *eykh*

how far כמה רחוק
kama rakhok

how long עוד כמה זמן
od kama zman

how many כמה *kama*

how much כמה *kama*

hug v לחבק *lekhabek*

hungry רעב / רעבה
ra-ev (m) / re-eva (f)

hunting צייד *tzayad*

hurry למהר
lemaher

hurt (v) לפגוע lifgo-a; (adj) פצוע / patzu-a (m) / ptzu-a (f) פצועה

husband בעל ba-al

I

I אני ani

ice קרח eerakh

icy (weather) קפוא kafu

identification (card) מסמך זיהוי mismakh zihuy

if אם im

ill [BE] חולֶה / חולָה khole (m) / khola (f)

illness מחלה makhala

important חשוב khashuv

imported מיובא meyuba

impressive מרשים / מרשימה marshim (m) / marshima (f)

in בתוך betokh

include כולל kolel

indoor מקורה mekure

inexpensive לא יקר lo yakar

infected מזוהם mezoham

infection זיהום zihum

inflammation דלקת daleket

information מידע meyda

information desk דוכן מודיעין dukhan modi'in

injection זריקה zrika

injure לפצוע liftzoa

injury פציעה ptzi-a

inn פונדק pundak

innocent חף מפשע / חפה מפשע khaf mipesha (m) / khafa mipesha (f)

inquiry שאלה sh'ela

insect bite עקיצה akitza

insect repellent דוחה חרקים dokheh kharakim

insect spray תרסיס נגד חרקים tarsis neged kharakim

inside בתוך betokh

instant messenger שירות הודעות מיידיות sherut hoda-ot miyadiyot

insurance ביטוח bitu-ach

insurance claim תביעת ביטוח tvi-at bitu-ach

interest (finance) ריבית ribit

interested מעוניין / מעוניינת me-unyan (m) / me-unyenet (f)

interesting מעניין / מעניינת me-anyen (m) / me-anyenet (f)

international ; (airport terminal) בינלאומי beynle-umi

international flight טיסה בינלאומית tisa beynle-umit

internet אינטרנט internet

internet cafe בית קפה אינטרנט beyt kafe internet

interpreter מתורגמן / מתורגמנית meturgeman (m) / meturgemanit (f)

intersection צומת *tzomet*

introduce להכיר *lehakir*

introduction (social) היכרות *heykerut*

investment השקעה *hashka'a*

invitation הזמנה *hazmana*

invite *v* להזמין *lehazmin*

invoice חשבונית *kheshbonit*

iodine יוד *yod*

Ireland אירלנד *irland*

Irish (person) אירי / אירית *iri (m) / irit (f)* ;
 adj מאירלנד *me-irland*

iron *n* **(clothing)**; *v* מגהץ לגהץ *maghetz legahetz*

itemized bill חשבון מפורט *kheshbon meforat*

J

jacket ז'קט *zhaket*

jar (container) צנצנת *tzintzenet*

jaw לסת *leset*

jazz ג'ז *jez*

jeans ג'ינס *jins*

jet ski אופנוע ים *ofanoa yam*

jeweler תכשיטן / תכשיטנית *takhshitan (m) / takhshitanit (f)*

join *v* להצטרף *lehitztaref*

joint (anatomy) מפרק *mifrak*

journey מסע *masa*

just (only) רק *rak*

K

keep להחזיק *lehakhzik*

kerosene קרוסין *kerosin*

key מפתח *mafte-akh*

key card כרטיס מפתח *kartis mafte-akh*

kiddie pool בריכה לילדים *breykha liyladim*

kidney כליה *kilya*

kilogram קילוגרם *kilogram*

kilometer קילומטר *kilometer*

kind *adj*; *n* טוב לב סוג *tuv lev sug*

kiss *v* לנשק *lenashek*

knee ברך *berekh*

knife סכין *sakin*

knitwear סריג *sarig*

knock לדפוק *lidfok*

know לדעת *lada-at*

L

label תווית *tavit*

lace תחרה *takhara*

lactose intolerant רגיש למוצרי חלב / רגישה למוצרי חלב *ragish lemutzarey khalav (m) / regisha lemutzarey khalav (f)*

lake אגם *agam*

lamp מנורה *menora*

landscape נוף *nof*

language שפה *safa*

lantern פנס *panas*

large גדול / גדולה
gadol (male) / gdola (female)

last (adj)
אחרון/אחרונה
(v) להישאר *lehisha-er*
akharon (m) / akhrona (f)

late (time) ; **(delay)**
מאוחר איחור
meukhar ikhur

laugh צחוק *tzkhok*

launderette [BE] מכבסה
makhbesa

laundromat מכבסה אוטומטית
makhbesa Otomatit

laundry כביסה *kvisa*

laundry facilities מתקני כביסה
mitkaney kvisa

laundry service שירות כביסה
sherut kvisa

lawyer עורך דין / עורכת דין
orekh din (m) / orekhet din (f)

laxative חומר משלשל
khomer meshalshel

leather עור *or*

leave v; **(behind)** לעזוב *la-azov*

left שמאל *smol*

left-luggage office [BE]
שירות שמירת חפצים
sherut shmirat khafatzim

leg רגל *regel*

lens (camera)
; **(glasses)** עדשה *adasha*

less פחות *pakhot*

lesson שיעור *she-ur*

letter מכתב *mikhtav*

library ספריה *sifriya*

license (driving) רישיון
rishayon

life boat סירת הצלה
sirat hatzala

life guard (beach) מציל
matzil

life jacket חגורת הצלה
khagorat hatzala

life preserver חגורת הצלה
khagorat hatzala

lift [BE] elevator מעלית
ma-alit

light (color) בהיר *bahir*;
(weight) קל *kal*

light bulb נורה *nura*

lighter מצית *matzit*

lightning ברק *barak*

like; **(please)** הצור / הצור
rotze (m) / rotza (f)

linen מצעים *matza-im*

lip שפה *safa*

lipstick שפתון *sfaton*

liquor store חנות משקאות חריפים
khanut mashka-ot kharifim

listen להקשיב *lehakshiv*

liter ליטר *liter*

little (amount) קצת *ktzat*

live *v* לחיות *likhyot*

loafers מוקסינים *mokasinim*

local מקומי *mekomi*

log off להתנתק *lehitnatek*

log on להתחבר *lehitkhaber*

login כניסה למערכת
knisa lama-arekhet

long ארוך *arokh*

long-sighted [BE]
רחוק-ראיה / רחוקת ראיה
rekhok re-ıya (m) /
rekhokat re-ıya (f)

look *v* להסתכל *lehistakel*

lose לאבד *le-abed*

loss אובדן *ovdan*

lost אבוד *avud*

lost and found מחלקת אבידות
makhleket avedot

lost property office [BE]
מחלקת אבידות
makhleket avedot

lotion תחליב *takhliv*

loud (voice) קולני *kolani*

love *v* לאהוב *le-ehov*

lovely מקסים *maksim*

low נמוך / נמוכה
namukh (m) / nemukha (f)

low tide שפל *shefel*

luck מזל *mazal*

luggage מטען *mitan*

luggage cart עגלת מזוודות
eglat mizvadot

luggage locker תא אחסון
ta ikhsun

lunch ארוחת צהריים
arukhat tzohora-im

lung ריאה *re-a*

M

magazine כתב עת *ktav et*

magnificent מקסים *maksim*

maid עוזרת בית *ozeret Ba-it*

mail *n* דואר *do-ar;* *v*
לשלוח בדואר
lishlo-akh bado-ar

mailbox תבת דואר *tevat do-ar*

make-up *n* רופיא *lpur*

mall קניון *kenyon*

mallet פטיש עץ *patish etz*

man גבר *gever*

manager מנהל / מנהלת
menahel (m) / menahelet (f)

manicure מניקור *manikur*

many רבים *rabim*

map מפה *mapa*

market *n* שוק *shuk*

married נשוי / נשואה
nasuy (m) / nesu-a (f)

mass (religious service) מיסה
misa

massage עיסוי *isuy*

match *n* (sport) תחרות *takharut*

material חומר *khomer*

matinée הצגה יומית *hatzaga yomit*

mattress מזרן *mizran*

may *v* אולי *ulay*

meadow אחו *akhu*

meal ארוחה *arukha*

mean *v* להתכוון *lehitkaven*

measure למדוד *limdod*

measuring cup כוס מדידה *kos medida*

measuring spoon כף מדידה *kaf medida*

mechanic מכונאי *mekhona-i*

medicine (drug) תרופה *trufa*

meet לפגוש *lifgosh*

memorial אזכרה *azkara*

memory card כרטיס זיכרון *kartis zikaron*

mend לתקן *letaken*

menu תפריט *tafrit*

message הודעה *hoda-a*

meter מטר *meter*

middle אמצע *emtza*

midnight חצות *khatzot*

mileage מרחק במיילים *merkhak bemaylim*

minute דקה *daka*

mirror מראה *mara*

miscellaneous שונות *shonot*

Miss עלמה *alma*

miss *v* (lacking) לפספס *lefasfes*

mistake טעות *ta-ut*

mobile phone [BE] טלפון סלולרי *telefon selolari*

moisturizing cream קרם לחות *krem lakhut*

moment רגע *rega*

money כסף *kesef*

money order המחאת דואר *hamkha-at do-ar*

month חודש *khodesh*

monument מצבת זיכרון *matzevat zikaron*

moon ירח *yare-akh*

mop *n* מגב *magav*

moped טוסטוס *tustus*

more עוד *od*

morning בוקר *boker*

mosque מסגד *misgad*

mosquito net רשת נגד יתושים *reshet neged yatushim*

motel מוטל *motel*

motorboat סירת מנוע *sirat manoa*

motorcycle אופנוע *ofano-a*

motorway [BE] כביש מהיר *kvish mahir*

moustache שפם *safam*

mouth פה *pe*

mouthwash מי פה *mey pe*

move v לזוז *lazuz*

movie סרט *seret*

Mr. מר *mar*

Mrs. גברת *geveret*

much הרבה *harbeh*

mug n ספל *sefel*

mugging לשדוד *lishdod*

muscle שריר *shrir*

museum מוזיאון *muze-on*

music מוסיקה *musika*

musical מחזמר *mukhazemer*

must (have to) חייב / חייבת
  khayav (m) / khayevet (f)

N

nail (body) ציפורן *tziporen*

nail clippers קוצץ ציפורניים
  kotzetz tziporna-im

nail file פצירת צפורניים *ptzirat*
  tziporna-im

nail salon סלון יופי *salon yofi*

name שם *shem*

napkin מפית *mapit*

nappy [BE] חיתול *khitul*

narrow צר *tzar*

nationality לאום *le-om*

natural טבעי *tivi*

nausea בחילה *bkhila*

near קרוב *karov*

nearby ליד *leyad*

near-sighted
  קצר ראיה / קצרת ראיה
  ktzar re-iya (m) / kitzrat re-iya (f)

neck צוואר *tzavar*

necklace מחרוזת *makhrozet*

need v להזדקק *lehizdakek*

needle מחט *makhat*

nerve עצב *etzev*

never לעולם לא *le-olam Lo*

new חדש *khadash*

newspaper עיתון *iton*

newsstand דוכן עיתונים
  dukhan itonim

next אבה *haba*

next to ליד *leyad*

nice (beautiful) נחמד
  nekhmad

night לילה *layla*

no לא *lo*

noisy רועש *ro-esh*

none אף אחד *af ekhad*

non-smoking לא מעשנים
  lo me-ashnim

noon צהריים *tzohora-im*

normal נורמלי *normali*

north צפון *tzafon*

nose אף *af*

not לא *lo*

note (bank note) שטר *shtar*

notebook מחברת *makhberet*

nothing כלום *klum*
notice (sign) הודעה *hoda-a*
notify להודיע *lehodi-a*
novice מתחיל / מתחילה
   matkhil (m) / matkhila (f)
now עכשיו *akhshav*
number מספר *mispar*
nurse אחות *akhot*

O

o'clock השעה *hasha-a*
occupation מקצוע *miktzo-a*
occupied תפוס *tafus*
office משרד *misrad*
off-licence [BE] מחוץ לרישיון
   mikhutz larishayon
oil שמן *shemen*
old ישן *yashan*
old town העיר העתיקה
   ha-ir ha-atika
on על *al*
on time בזמן *bazman*
once פעם אחת *pa-am akhat*
one-way ticket כרטיס הלוך
   kartis halokh
only רק *rak*
open *adj* פתוח *patu-akh*; *v* לפתוח
   lifto-akh
opera אופרה *opera*
operation תפעול *tif-ul*
operator מפעיל *mafil*
opposite ההפך *hahefekh*

optician אופטיקאי *optika-i*
or או *o*
orange (color) כתום *katom*
orchestra תזמורת *tizmoret*
order *n* תלצוות *tzav* [decree]; *v* צו;
   סדר *seder* [tidy]; *letzavot*
out of order מקולקל
   mekulkal
out of stock אזל מהמלאי
   azal mehamelay
outlet (electric) שקע חשמלי
   sheka khashmali
outside בחוץ *bakhutz*
oval סגלגל *sgalgal*
overlook *n* תצפית *taztzpit*
oxygen treatment טיפול עם חמצן
   åtipul im khamtzan

P

pacifier (baby's) מוצץ
   motzetz
packet חפיסה *hhafisa*
pad (sanitary) תחבושת
   takhboshet
pail דלי *dli*
pain כאב *ke-ev*
painkiller משכך כאבים
   meshakech Ke-evim
paint *n*; *v* צבע לצבוע
   tzeva litzboa
painting צביעה *tzvi-a*
pair זוג *zug*

pajamas פיג׳מה *pijama*

palace ארמון *armon*

palpitations פלפיטציה *palpitatzia*

pants מכנסיים *mikhnasayim*

panty hose גרבונים *garbonim*

paper נייר *neyar*

paper towel מגבת נייר *magevet neyar*

parcel [BE] חבילה *khavila*

parents הורים *horim*

park n פארק *;* park *;* v לחנות *lakhanot*

parking חניה *khanaya*

parking disc תו חניה *tav khanaya*

parking garage חניה מקורה *khanaya mekora*

parking lot מגרש חניה *migrash khanaya*

parking meter מדחן *madkhan*

part חלק *khelek*

part-time חלקי *khelki*

party (social gathering) מסיבה *mesiba*

passport דרכון *darkon*

passport control ביקורת דרכונים *bikoret darkonim*

passport photo תמונת פספורט *tmunat pasport*

paste (glue) להדביק *lehadbik*

pastry shop קונדיטוריה *konditurya*

patch טלאי *tlay*

path דרך *derekh*

patient מטופל / מטופלת *metupal (m) / metupelet (f)*

pattern דפוס *dfus*

pay לשלם *leshalem*

payment תשלום *tashlum*

peak n **(mountain)** פסגה *pisga*

pearl פנינה *pnina*

pedestrian הולך רגל *holekh regel*

pediatrician רופא ילדים / רופאת ילדים *rofe yeladim (m) / rofat yeladim (f)*

pedicure פדיקור *pedikur*

peg (tent) יתד *yated*

pen עט *rt*

pencil עיפרון *iparon*

pendant תליון *talyon*

penicillin פניצילין *penitzilin*

per day ליום *leyom*

per hour לשעה *lesha-ah*

per person לאדם *le-adam*

per week לשבוע *leshavu-ah*

percentage אחוז *akhuz*

perfume בושם *bosem*

perhaps אולי *ulay*

period (monthly) מחזור *makhzor*

permit n (fishing) ; (hunting) היתר heyter

person אדם adam

personal אישי ishi

petite קטנה ktana

petrol [BE] דלק delek

pewter פיוטר pyuter

pharmacy בית מרקחת beyt mirkakhat

phone card כרטיס חיוג kartis khiyug

photo תמונה tmuna

photocopy n צילום tzilum

photograph n תמונה tmuna

photography צילום tzilum

phrase ביטוי bituy

pick up v (go get) לקבל lekabel

picnic פיקניק piknik

picnic basket סלסלת פיקניק salsalat piknik

piece חתיכה khatikha

pill גלולה glula

pillow כרית karit

PIN קוד סודי kod sodi

pin n (brooch) סיכה sika

pink ורוד varod

pipe מקטרת mikteret

place n מקום makom

plane fly מטוס matos

planetarium מצפה כוכבים mitzpe kokhavim

plaster [BE] (bandage) פלסטר plaster

plastic פלסטיק plastik

plastic bag שקית ניילון dakit naylon

plastic wrap ניילון נצמד naylon nitzmad

plate צלחת tzalakhat

platform [BE] (station) רציף ratzif

platinum פלטינה platina

play n הצגה hatzaga (theatre) ; v לשחק lesakhek

playground מגרש משחקים migrash miskhakim

playpen לול lul

please בבקשה bevakasha

plug (electric) תקע חשמלי teka Khashmali

plunger פומפה pompa

pneumonia דלקת ריאות daleket re-ot

pocket כיס kis

point of interest נקודת עניין nekudat inyan

point v להצביע lehatzbi-a

poison רעל ra-al

poisoning הרעלה harala

pole (ski); (tent) מוט mot

police משטרה mishtara

police report דו"ח משטרתי dokh mishtarti

police station תחנת משטרה
takhanat mishtara

pond אגם *agam*

pool בריכה *brekha*

porcelain חרסינה *kharsina*

port נמל *namal*

portable נישא *nisa*

porter סבל *sabal*

portion חלק *khelek*

post [BE] *n* דואר *do-ar; v* לשלוח
בדואר *lishlo-akh bado-ar*

post office משרד הדואר
misrad hado-ar

postage דמי ביול *dmey biyul*

postage stamp בול דואר
bul do-ar

postcard גלויה *gluya*

pot סיר *sir*

pottery כלי חרס *kli kheres*

pound (British currency, weight)
פאונד *pa-und*

powder אבקה *avka*

pregnant בהריון *beherayon*

premium (gas/ petrol) פרימיום
primyum

prescribe לתת במרשם
latet bemirsham

prescription מרשם *mirsham*

present *n* מתנה *matana*

press (iron) גיהוץ בקיטור
gihutz bekitor

pressure לחץ *lakhatz*

pretty יפה / יפה
yafe (m) / yafa (f)

price מחיר *mekhir*

price-fixed menu
תפריט במחיר קבוע
tafrit bemekhir kavu-a

print *n* **(photo)** תדפיס *tadpis ; v*
(document) להדפיס
lehadpis

private פרטי *prati*

profit *n* רווח *revakh*

program (of events) תוכנית
tokhnit

pronounce *v* להגות
lahagot

pronunciation *n* הגיה *hagiya*

provide לספק *lesapek*

pull *v* למשוך *limshokh*

pump משאבה *masheva*

puncture פנצ'ר *pancher*

purchase *n* קניה *kniya;*
v לקנות *liknot*

pure טהור *tahor*

purple סגול *sagol*

purse (handbag) תיק יד
tik Yad

push *v* דחוף *lidkhof*

pushchair [BE] עגלת ילדים
eglat Yeladim

put לשים *lasim*

Q

quality איכות *eykhut*

quantity כמות *kamut*

question n שאלה *she-ela*

quick מהר *maher*

quiet שקט *shaket*

R

race מירוץ *meyrotz*

race track מסלול המירוצים
maslul hameyrotzim

racket (sport) מחבט *makhbet*

radio רדיו *radyo*

railway station [BE] תחנת רכבת
takhanat rakevet

rain גשם *geshem*

raincoat מעיל גשם
me-il geshem

rape n אונס *ones*

rash פריחה *prikha*

rate n **(exchange) ; (price)** תעריף
ta-arif

razor סכין גילוח
sakin gilu-akh

razor blade סכין גילוח
sakin gilu-akh

ready מוכן / מוכנה
mukhan (m) / mukhana (f)

real (genuine) אמיתי *amiti*

rear מאחור *me-akhor*

receipt קבלה *kabala*

reception קבלה *kabala*

receptionist פקידת קבלה
pkidat kabala

recommend להמליץ *lehamlitz*

rectangular מלבני *malbeni*

red אדום *adom*

reduction הפחתה *hafkhata*

refrigerator מקרר *mekarer*

refund v להחזיר *lehakhzir*

regards n הערכה *ha-arakha;* v
להתייחס *lehityakhes*

region איזור *ezor*

registered mail דואר רשום
do-ar rashum

registration הרשמה *harshama*

regular (gas / petrol) רגיל *ragil*

relationship מערכת יחסים
ma-arekhet yakhasim

reliable אמין *amin*

religion דת *dat*

rent v לשכור *liskor*

rental השכרה *haskara*

rental car מכונית שכורה
mekhonit skhura

repair n תיקון *tikun;*
v לתקן *letaken*

repeat לחזור v *lakhazor*

report (theft) לדווח
ledaveakh

request n בקשה *bakasha;* v לבקש
levakesh

required דרוש *darush*

requirement דרישה *drisha*

reservation הזמנה *hazmana*

reservations office משרד הזמנות
misrad hazmanot

reserve לשמור *lishmor*

reserved שמור *shmor*

rest n מנוחה *menukha*

restaurant מסעדה *misada*

restroom שירותים *sherutim*

retired adj גמלאי / גמלאית
gimla-I (m)/gimla-it (f);
לצאת לגמלאות ; *latzet legimla-ot* v

return (come back); (give back)
לחזור; להחזיר
lakhazor; lehakhzir

return ticket [BE]
כרטיס הלוך\כרטיס הלוך חזור
kartis halokh/kartis halokh khazur

rib צלע *tzela*

ribbon סרט **seret**

right (correct) נכון *nakhon;*
(direction) ימין *yamin*

ring (jewelry) טבעת *taba-at*
ring (bell) לצלצל *letzaltzel*

river נהר *nahar*

road דרך *derekh*

road assistance שירותי דרך
sherutey Derekh

road map מפת דרכים
mapat drakhim

road sign תמרור *tamrur*

robbery שוד *shod*

romantic רומנטי *romanti*

room (hotel); (space) חדר ; מקום
kheder; makom

room number מספר חדר
mispar kheder

room service שירות חדרים
sherut khadarim

room temperature
טמפרטורה בחדר
temperatura bakheder

rope חבל *khevel*

round עגול *agol*

round (golf) סבב *sevev*

round-trip ticket
כרטיס הלוך ושוב
kartis halokh vashov

route נתיב *nativ*

rowboat סירת משוטים
sirat meshotim

rubber (material) גומי *gumi*

rubbish [BE] זבל *zevel*

ruby אודם *odem*

S

Sabbath שַׁבָּת *shabbat*

safe n (vault) כספת *kasefet*; **(not in
danger)** בטוח / בטוחה
batu-akh (m) / betukha (f)

safety pin סיכת ביטחון
sikat bitakhon

sailboat סירת מפרש *sirat mifras*

sale n; **(bargains)** במבצע bemivtza

same אותו דבר oto davar

sand חול khol

sandal סנדל sandal

sanitary napkin
תחבושת היגיינית
takhboshet higiyenit

sapphire ספיר sapir

satin סטן saten

saucepan סיר sir

saucer צלוחית tzlokhit

sauna סאונה sa-una

save v לשמור lishmor **[guard]**;
לחסוך lakhasokh **[money]**;
להציל lehatzil **[lives]**

savings account חשבון חיסכון
kheshbon khisakhon

scarf צעיף tza-if

scenery נוף nof

scenic route דרך נוף derekh nof

school בית ספר beyt sefer

scissors מספריים mispara-im

scooter קטנוע katnoa

Scotland סקוטלנד Skotland

screwdriver מברג mavreg

sculpture פסל pesel

sea ים yam

season עונה ona

seat מושב moshav

seat belt חגורת בטיחות
khagorat betikhut

second n שניה shniya;
adj נוסף nosaf

second class סוג ב' sug bet

second-hand shop
חנות יד שניה
khanut yad shniya

section סעיף sa-if

see לראות lirot

sell למכור limkor

send לשלוח lishloakh

senior citizen גמלאי / גמלאית
gimla-i (m) / gimla-it (f)

sentence משפט mishpat

separated (relationship)
פרוד / פרודה
parud (m) / pruda (f)

serious רציני / רצינית
retzini (m) / retzinit (f)

serve (meal) להגיש lehagish

service (restaurant) שירות
sherut

set menu תפריט קבוע
tafrit kavu-a

sew לתפור litfor

shampoo שמפו shampo

shape לעצב le-atzev

sharp (pain) חד khad

shave n להתגלח lehitgale-akh

shaving brush מברשת גילוח
mivreshet giluakh

shaving cream קרם גילוח
krem giluakh

shelf מדף madaf

ship n v אוניה לשלוח
oniya lishlo-akh

shirt חולצה khultza

shoe נעל na-al

shoe store חנות נעליים
khanut na-alayim

shop n חנות khanut

shopping קניות kniyot

shopping area אזור קניות
ezor kniyot

shopping centre [BE] מרכז קניות
merkaz kniyot

shopping mall קניון kenyon

short קצר / קצרה
katzar (m) / ktzara (f)

shorts מכנסיים קצרים
mikhnasa-im ktzarim

short-sighted [BE]
קצר ראיה / קצרת ראיה
ktzar re-iya (m) / kitzrat re-iya (f)

shoulder כתף katef

shovel n את et

show n; v הופעה הופיע
hofa-ah lehofi-a

shower (stall) מקלחת miklakhat

shrine מזבח mizbe-akh

shut v לסגור lisgor;
סגור / סגורה n
sagur (m) /sgura (f)

shutter (window) תריס tris

side צד tzad

sightseeing תיירות
tayarut

sightseeing tour נסיעת תיירות
nesi-at tayarut

sign שלט shelet

sign (notice) v לאותת le-otet

signature חתימה khatima

silk משי meshi

silver כסף kesef

silverware כלי כסף kley kesef

since מאז me-az

sing לשיר lashir

single n (ticket) בודד boded;
(unmarried)
רווק / רווקה ravak (m) / ravaka (f)

single room חדר לאחד
kheder le-echad

size; (clothes); (shoes) גודל
godel

skate v להחליק lehakhlik

skating rink רחבת החלקה
rakhavat hakhlaka

skin עור or

skirt חצאית khatzait

sky שמיים shamayim

sleep v לישון lishon

sleeping bag שק שינה
sak shena

sleeping car קרון שינה
karon shena

sleeping pill גלולת שינה
glulat shena

sleeve שרוול *sharvul*

slice n חתיכה *khatikha*

slide (photo) שקופית *shikufit*

slipper נעל בית *na-al bayit*

slow לאט *le-at*

small קטן / קטנה
katan (m) / ktana (f)

smoke n; v עשן; לעשן
ashan; leashen

smoker מעשן / מעשנת
me-ashen (m) / me-ashenet (f)

snack חטיף *khatif*

snack bar מזנון *miznon*

sneaker נעל התעמלות
na-al hitamlut

snorkeling equipment
ציוד שנורקלינג
tziyud snorkeling

snow שלג *sheleg*

soap סבון *sabon*

soccer כדורגל *kaduregel*

soccer match משחק כדורגל
miskhak kaduregel

sock גרב *gerev*

socket (electric) תושבת *toshevet*

soft רך / רכה
rakh (m) / raka (f)

sold out אזל מהמלאי
azal mehamelay

someone מישהו / מישהי
mishehu (m) / mishehi (f)

something משהו *mashehu*

song שיר *shir*

soon בקרוב *bekarov*

sore (painful) כואב *ko-ev*

sore throat כאב גרון *ke-ev Garon*

sorry סליחה *slikha*

sort (kind) מעין *me-eyn*

south דרום *darom*

souvenir מזכרת *mazkeret*

souvenir shop חנות מזכרות
khanut mazkarot

spa ספא *spa*

spatula מרית *marit*

speak v לדבר *ledaber*

special מיוחד / מיוחדת
meyukhad (m) / meyukhedet (f)

specialist מומחה *mumkhe*

speciality התמחות *hitmakhut*

spell v לאיית *le-ayet*

spend לבזבז *levazbez*

spine עמוד שדרה *amud shidra*

sponge ספוג *sfog*

spoon כף *kaf*

sport ספורט *sport*

sporting goods store
חנות מוצרי ספורט
khanut mutzrey sport

sprained נקוע / נקועה
naku-a (m) / neku-a (f)

square (shape) מרובע *meruba*

stadium איצטדיון *itztadyon*

staff סגל *segel*

stain כתם *ketem*

stainless steel פלדת אל חלד
pladat al kheled

stairs מדרגות
madregot

stamp n **(postage)**; v **(ticket)**
בול להחתים
bul lehakhtim

staple לשדך *leshadekh*

star כוכב *kokhav*

start v; n התחילה; התחלה
lehatkhil; hatkhala

starter [BE] (meal)
מנה ראשונה
mana rishona

station (train); (subway)
תחנה *takhana*

stationery store
חנות למכשירי כתיבה
khanut lemakhshirey ktiva

stay (trip) שהות *shahut*;
v **(remain)** להישאר *lehisha-er*;
v **(reside)** לגור *lagur*

steal לגנוב *lignov*

sterling silver כסף סטרלינג
kesef sterling

sting n; v עוקץ לעקוץ
oketz la-akotz

stockings גרביונים
garbiyonim

stomach קיבה *keva*

stomachache כאב בטן
ke-ev beten

stop (bus); v **stop**
תחנה לעצור
takhana la-atzor

store (shop) חנות *khanut*

store directory מדריך חנויות
madrikh khanuyot

stove תנור *tanur*

straight ahead ישר *yashar*

strange מוזר *muzar*

street רחוב *rehov*

street map מפות רחובות
mapat rehovot

string חוט *khut*

stroller עגלת ילדים
eglat yeladim

strong חזק / חזקה
khazak (m) / khazaka (f)

student סטודנט / סטודנטית
student (m) / studentit (f)

study v ללמוד *lilmod*

stunning מהמם *mehamem*

sturdy בנוי היטב *banuy heytev*

subway רכבת תחתית
rakevet takhtit

subway map מפת רכבת תחתית
mapat rakevet takhtit

suit (man's); (woman's) חליפה
khalifa

suitcase מזוודה *mizvada*

sun שמש *shemesh*

sunburn כוויה *kviya*

sunglasses משקפי שמש
mishkefey shemesh

sunstroke מכת שמש
makat shemesh

sun-tan lotion תחליב שיזוף
takhliv shizuf

super (gas/ petrol) סופר *super*

supermarket סופרמרקט
supermarket

supplement *n* תוסף *tosaf*

suppository פתילה *ptila*

surgery [BE] ניתוח *nitu-akh*

surname שם משפחה
shem mishpakha

swallow לבלוע *livlo-a*

sweater סוודר *sveder*

sweatshirt סווטשירט
svetshert

sweet מתוק / מתוקה
matok (m) / metuka (f)

swell להתנפח
lehitnape-akh

swelling התנפחות
hitnapkhut

swim *v* לשחות *liskhot*

swimming שחיה *skhiya*

swimming pool בריכת שחיה
brekhat skhiya

swimming trunks מכנסי רחצה
mikhnasey rakhatza

swollen נפוח *nafu-akh*

symbol סמל *semel*

synagogue בית כנסת
beyt Kneset

synthetic סינתטי *sinteti*

system מערכת *ma-arekhet*

T

table שולחן *shulkhan*

tablet (medical) טבליה *tavlia*

tailor חייט *khayat*

take לקחת *lakakhat*

take away *v* [BE] לקחת
lakakhat

taken (occupied) תפוס *tafus*

tampon טמפון *tampon*

tap (water) ברז *terez*

tax מס *mas*

taxi מונית *monit*

taxi rank [BE] תחנת מוניות
takhanat moniyot

taxi stand תחנת מוניות
takhanat moniyot

team צוות *tzevet*

tear *v* לקרוע *likro-a*

teaspoon כפית *kapit*

telephone booth תא טלפון
ta Telefon

telephone directory
מדריך טלפונים
madrikh Telefonim

telephone n; v
טלפון לטלפן *relefon letalpen*

telephone number מספר טלפון
mispar telefon

tell לומר *lomar*

temperature טמפרטורה
temperatura

temple מקדש *mikdash*

temporary זמני *zmani*

tennis court מגרש טניס
migrash tenis

tennis match משחק טניס
miskhak tenis

tennis racket מחבט טניס
makhvet tenis

tent אוהל *ohel*

tent peg יתד אוהל *yated ohel*

tent pole מוט אוהל
mot ohel

terminal טרמינל, מסוף
terminal, masof

terrace טרסה *terasa*

terrible נורא *nora*

terrifying מפחיד *mafkhid*

thank להודות *lehodot*

thank you תודה *toda*

theater תיאטרון *te-atron*

theft גניבה *gneva*

then אז *az*

there שם *sham*

thermometer מדחום
madkhom

thief גנב *ganav*

thigh ירך *yarekh*

thin רזֶה / רזָה
raze (m) / raza (f)

think (believe) חושב / חושבת
khoshev (m) / khoshevet (f)

thirsty צמא / צמאה
tzame (m) / tzme-a (f)

thread חוט *khut*

throat גרון *garon*

through דרך *derekh*

thumb אגודל *agudal*

thunder רעם *ra-am*

thunderstorm
סופת רעמים
sufat re-amim

ticket כרטיס *kartis*

ticket office משרד כרטיסים
misrad kartisim

tide גאות *ge-ut*

tie v לקשור *likshor;*
n *aniva* עניבה

tie clip הביגע תכיס *sikat aniva*

time n ; (recurrent occasion)
מועד *mo-ed*

timetable [BE] לוח זמנים
lu-akh zmanim

tin [BE] (container) קופסת שימורים
kufsat shimurim

tin opener [BE] פותחן שימורים
potkhan shimurim

tire צמיג *tzamig*

tired עייף / עייפה
ayef (m) / ayefa (f)

tissue ממחטת נייר
mimkhetet neyar

to אל *el*

tobacco טבק *tabak*

tobacconist בעל חנות טבק
ba-al khanut tabak

today היום *hayom*

toe בוהן *bohen*

toilet [BE] שירותים *herutim*

toilet paper נייר טואלט
neyar to-alet

toiletry תמרוקים
amrukim

tomb קבר *kever*

tomorrow מחר *makhar*

tongue לשון *lashon*

tonight הלילה *halayla*

too (also) גם *gam*

too much יותר מדי
yoter miday

tool כלי *kli*

tooth שן *shen*

toothache כאב שיניים
ke-ev shinayim

toothbrush מברשת שיניים
mivreshet shinayim

toothpaste משחת שיניים
mishkhat shinayim

Torah תּוֹרָה *torah*

torn (clothes) קרוע *karu-a*

touch v לגעת *laga-at*

tour טיול *tiyul*

tourist office משרד תיירות
misrad tayarut

tow truck גרר *grar*

towards לכיוון *lekivun*

towel מגבת *magevet*

tower מגדל *migdal*

town עיירה *ayara*

town hall בית העירייה
beyt ha-irya

toy צעצוע *tza-atzu-a*

toy store חנות צעצועים
khanut tza-atzu-im

track (train) מסילה *mesila*

traffic light רמזור *ramzor*

trail שביל *shvil*

trailer טריילר *treyler;*
נגרר *nigrar*

train רכבת *rakevet*

tram רכבת קלה *Rakevet kala*

tranquillizer חומר מרגיע
khomer margi-a

transfer (money) העברה
ha-avara

translate לתרגם *letargem*

travel לנסוע *linso-a*

travel agency סוכנות נסיעות
sokhnut nesi-ot

travel guide
מדריך טיולים / מדריכת טיולים
madrikh tiyulim (m) / madrikhat tiyulim (f)

travel sickness מחלת נסיעה
makhalat nesi-a

traveler's check המחאת נוסעים
humkha-at nosim

treatment טיפול *tipul*

tree עץ *etz*

trim לגזום *liqzom*

trip נסיעה *nesi-a*

trolley חשמלית *khasmalit*

trousers [BE] מכנסיים
mikhnasa-im

T-shirt חולצת טריקו
khultzat triko

tube שפופרת *shfoferet*

turn (change direction) לפנות
lifnot

turtleneck צוארון גולף
tzavaron golf

TV טלביזיה *televizya*

tweezers פינצטה *pintzeta*

U

ugly מכוער **mekho-ar**

umbrella מטריה *mitriya*;
(beach) שמשיה *shimshiya*

unconscious
מחוסר הכרה / מחוסרת הכרה
*mekhusar hakara (m) /
mekhuseret hakara (f)*

under מתחת *mitakhat*

underground station [BE]
תחנת רכבת תחתית
takhanat rakevet takhtit

underpants תחתונים
takhtonim

undershirt גופיה *gufiya*

understand להבין *lehavin*

undress להתפשט
lehitpashet

United States ארצות הברית
srtzot habrit

university אוניברסיטה
universita

unleaded (fuel) נטול עופרת
netul oferet

until עד *ad*

up למעלה *lemala*

upstairs בקומה למעלה
bakoma lemala

urgent דחוף *dakhuf*

use להשתמש
lehishtamesh

usually בדרך כלל
bederekh klal

V

vacancy חדר פנוי
kheder panuy

vacant פנוי *panuy*

vacation חופשה *khufsha*

vaccinate לחסן
lekhasen

vacuum cleaner שואב אבק
shoev avak

valley עמק *emek*

value ערך *erekh*

value-added tax [BE]
מס ערך מוסף
mas erekh musaf

vegetarian
צמחוני / צמחונית
tzimkhoni (m) / tzimkhonit (f)

vein וריד *vrid*

very מאוד *meod*

veterinarian וטרינר / וטרינרית
veterinar (m) / veterinarit (f)

video camera מצלמת וידיאו
matzlemat video

view (panorama) נוף *nof*

village כפר *kfar*

visit *n* ביקור *bikur;*
לבקר *v levaker*

visiting hours שעות ביקור
shot bikur

visually impaired לקויי ראיה
lekuyey re-iya

V-neck מחשוף וי *makhsof vi*

volleyball game
משחק כדור עף
mishkhak kadur af

voltage וולטז' *voltazh*

vomit *v* להקיא *lehaki*

W

wait *v* לחכות *lehakot*

waiter מלצר *meltzar*

waiting room חדר המתנה
kheder hamtana

waitress מלצרית
meltzarit

wake להתעורר *lehitorer*

wake-up call שיחת השכמה
sikhat hashkama

Wales וויילס *wels*

walk *n* הליכה *halikha*

wall קיר *kir*

wallet ארנק *arnak*

want לרצות *lirtzot*

warm (temperature) חמים *khamim;*
v **(reheat)** לחמם *lekhamem*

wash לרחוץ *lirkhotz*

washing machine מכונת כביסה
mekhonat kvisa

watch *n* שעון *sha-on*

water מים *mayim*

waterfall מפל *mapal*

waterproof (clothing)
מעיל גשם me-il geshem
(literally) מעיל גשם
amid bemayim

water-ski סקי מים
ski mayim

wave n גל gal

way דרך derekh

weather מזג אוויר
mezeg avir

weather forecast
תחזית מזג אוויר
takhazit mezeg avir

week שבוע shavu-a

weekend סופשבוע
sofshavu-a

well באר be-er

west מערב ma-arav

what מה ma

wheel גלגל galgal

wheelchair כסא גלגלים
kise galgalim

when מתי matay

where איפה eyfo

which איזה eyze

white לבן lavan

who מי mi

whole שלם shalem

why למה lama

wide רחב / רחבה
rakhav (m) / rekhava (f)

widow (f) אלמנה almana;
(m) אלמן alman

wife אישה isha

WiFi Wifi Wi-Fi

wind רוח ru-akh

window; (shop) חלון ראווה
khalon ra-ava

window seat מושב חלון
moshav khalon

windsurfer גלישת רוח
glishat ru-akh

wine list רשימת יינות
reshimat yeynot

wireless אלחוטי alkhuti

wish v לאחל le-akhel

with עם im

withdraw (banking) למשוך
limshokh

without ללא lelo

woman אישה isha

wonderful נהדר / נהדרת
nehedar (m) / nehederet (f)

wood עץ etz

wool צמר tzemer

word מילה mila

work v לעבוד la-avod

worse גרוע יותר
garu-a yoter

wound פצע petza

write לכתוב likhtov

wrong לא נכון lo nakhon

X

X-ray רנטגן *rentgen*

Y

yacht יאכטה *yakhta*
year שנה *shana*
yellow צהוב *tzahov*
yes כן *ken*
yesterday אתמול *etmol*
yet עדיין *adayin*

young צעיר / צעירה
tza-ir (m) / tze-ira (f)
youth hostel אכסניית נוער
akhsaniyat no-ar

Z

zero אפס *efes*
zip(per) רוכסן *rukhsan*
zoo גן חיות *gan khayot*
zucchini קישוא *kishu*

NEXT TIME YOU TRAVEL, PACK A BERLITZ

BERLITZ PHRASE BOOKS
Communicate easily in over 30 languages

BERLITZ HANDBOOKS
Over 300 pages of comprehensive advice for inspiration, planning and on-the-ground use

BERLITZ POCKET GUIDES
The world's best-selling pocket guides, available for over 125 destinations worldwide

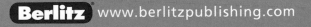
www.berlitzpublishing.com

Berlitz®

speaking your language

**phrase book & dictionary
phrase book & CD**

Available in: Arabic, Burmese*, Cantonese Chinese, Croatian, Czech*, Danish*, Dutch, English, Filipino, Finnish*, French, German, Greek, Hebrew*, Hindi*, Hungarian*, Indonesian, Italian, Japanese, Korean, Latin American Spanish, Malay, Mandarin Chinese, Mexican Spanish, Norwegian, Polish, Portuguese, Romanian*, Russian, Spanish, Swedish, Thai, Turkish, Vietnamese
*Book only

www.berlitzpublishing.com